How Harv a

MW01503589
have shaped people s lives

'The journey towards authenticity takes courage and vulnerability.
Harv embraces both as he chases his dream—shattering myths and
popular opinion along the way.'

Margaret Kouvelis, Executive Director, Talent Central

'Ian Harvey is your favourite leader's favourite leader. His raw authenticity
matched with decades of cutting-edge practice make this a must-read
for leaders who want to develop empathy and resilience. Harv has a mind
like no other—and his insights are gold for leaders who understand
that building empathy and making sense of complexity are the key
to finding success.

When I think about the lessons that have defined my 20's, almost all of
them have come from Ian Harvey. Harv's outlook on the world has taught
me so much—to have it distilled onto paper is a goldmine.'

Finn Shewell, Creator of SureMesh

'Harv is an unstoppable force of nature. A blunt Kiwi man-of-the-land
demeanour conceals a great intellect and mastery of how people really
work. He understands better than anyone else how to use the cumulative
brain power of individuals to achieve things beyond their expectations.
Ignore this book at your peril.'

Ian McDougall, Founder, Business Genetics

'Ian Harvey is an affable, mischievous disrupter. While you're on the roof
of your house admiring the view, he'll quietly remove the ladder.
He revels in encouraging you to get comfortable with being
uncomfortable. This reflects his paradox and his need to understand the
world around him, fuelled by what that knowledge might reveal.
This tension stimulates Harv's curiosity.'

Tony Gaskin, CEO Sympatico

'The combination of Harv's irreverence and multiple lives, will be sure to make this a great read.'
Andrea De Almada, Founder of ADA Advisory

'This man has a craft, one that I cherish and value deeply. Thanks Harv for being vulnerable for us to connect fully. I'm expecting the same vulnerability in this book allowing more people to connect.'
Catherine Van Der Meulen, Co Founder of Girls Who Grow

'Rach and I were catching up for a coffee with a paisley shirted gentleman with a striking haircut—a Purple Cow, as it were. It was hard to know what to expect, and the slight discomfort I felt on that day was a forewarning for how I'd feel as Harv pushed me to grow over my decade as a CQ member.

Many times entrepreneurs overlook the importance of timing in business, but timing is critical. For me, the timing of Harv and CQ bumping into me over a coffee at Café Cuba was spot on; any earlier and I wouldn't have been open to the challenge and any later and I wouldn't have been able to catch the wave that being a CQ member was for my development as a person and as a leader.'
James McCarthy Toia, Founder of Spidertracks and Cradle

'Over the last few years, I have invited Harv to join various leadership programmes as a (very reluctant) guest speaker. The insights he offers around unflinching self-reflection, and what's possible when you look honestly at the less comfortable aspects of your own thinking is inspirational. If you want to grow, develop, improve as a human, this is gold.'
Sarah Tocker, coach, facilitator and leadership specialist

'I've literally no idea what's in this book but if it's about Ian 'Bloody' Harvey, it can only be a fascinating read.'
Anake Goodall, Seed the Change

'The Collective Intelligence method supports exactly what it says: Collective Intelligence! My personal experience as a leader enabled me to use the wisdom and experience of my colleagues in the group to grow my leadership awareness, stretch and goals. This book is a valuable tool in the leadership toolbox.'

Robyn Shearer, Deputy Chief Executive, Health New Zealand

'An earthy bloke, who discovered that to be salt of the earth would take resilience, reinvention and reorientation of himself and those who choose to take the journey with him.

Harv is not afraid to call out what he sees as wrong, sometimes puts both feet in his mouth, and then with innate ability reflects, learns and shares how we can all be more decent humans to ourselves, each other, and the land we inhabit.'

Rev. David A. van Oeveren

'Collective Intelligence is about building emotional and relational capacity—attuning with others, the wider world, and the self. In a complex, remarkable, and changing world, these capacities would seem to me to be so very important. Harv brought something quite magical into being through Collective Intelligence—we would all benefit from more of the encounters, experiences, and insights it conjures.'

Alex Hannant, Director of Pocketknife

'Collective Intelligence has been a big part of my personal and professional growth over the past 10 years. It's a process that takes time but with that time comes huge reward. It takes you places that the standard course based process doesn't. We as a company are excited to see where the Work Place Impact Teams lead us, and I am excited to be part of that journey.'

Jamie Storey, CEO, ChemCare

As It Turns Out—No One's Got Their Shit Together: Learnings from inside the Collective Intelligence journey

Ian Harvey
PO Box 194
Feilding
Manawatū 4740
Aotearoa New Zealand

ISBN 978-1-0670528-0-5
Copyright © Ian Harvey 2025

Enquiries should be made to the author, Ian Harvey.
www.collectiveintelligence.co.nz

The author has performed in good faith, a diligent search to identify and locate the owner of all work quoted in this book before publication. The author has endeavoured to reference any work quoted in this book to the original owner and where appropriate and/or extensive, contacted same for their approval.

National Library of New Zealand
Cataloguing-in-publication data:
Creator: Harvey, Ian, author.
Title: As It Turns Out—No One's Got Their Shit Together: Learnings from inside the Collective Intelligence Journey / Ian Harvey.

ISBN: 978-1-0670528-0-5 (paperback)
Dewey No. 303
Notes: Includes bibliographical references.

Subjects:
Human Connected Eco-Systems
Authenticity
Consciousness
Paradigm shifts
Leadership
Collective Intelligence
High Performing Teams

Cover design by: Hannah Boom www.hannahboom.com
Editor: Bob Selden www.bobselden.com
Proof Editor: Intelligent Ink www.intelligentink.co.nz
Publisher: Collective Intelligence. Feilding, NZ. January 2025.
www.collectiveintelligence.co.nz

As It Turns Out—

No One's Got Their Sh*t Together

Learnings from inside the Collective Intelligence journey

Ian 'Harv' Harvey

Contents

Dedicating this book to the biggest influence in my life   9

Foreword   10

Introduction   13

Chapter 1   19

Influences are forever, even though the impact they have can be modified—
Thankfully, it doesn't matter if you haven't got your shit together—yet

Chapter 2   45

Why Authenticity Has Always Been a Fascination for Me—
Authenticity: The unspoken secret of good relationships

Chapter 3   52

From Shepherd to Uni Student—
Go do what others won't do and you'll succeed

Chapter 4   59

The Rag Trade is Bloody Tough—
When authenticity is all you have in the tool kit

Chapter 5   69

The Rob Moodie Effect—
Values and critical rigour define effective decisions

Chapter 6   76

Collective Intelligence: Origins and Defining Moments—
Don't pretend you've got your shit together—admit vulnerability

Chapter 7   82

Collective Intelligence: The Early Stages—
The power of collective minds

Chapter 8   86

Early CQ: The Powers of Listening and Emotional Intelligence—
Being actively quiet provides true focus

Chapter 9   94

Fuck, Harv, has no one got their shit together?—
Is the pain of failure too high to face up to reality?

Chapter 10   97

Our Backward Bureaucracy—
Is efficiency different to innovation? Is one way more valuable
than the other?

Chapter 11   102

Diversity Started to Raise its Head—
The power of different thinking

Chapter 12   108

Building Your Personal Base—
And having external, invigorating interests is also important to
your well-being

Chapter 13   115

The Need to Upskill in the face of Diversity Span—
Is Number 8 wire the answer?

Chapter 14   124

**Doing Business for the Sake of Shareholder Returns Only
is One Way to Fuck the Planet Quickly—**
How will future generations have the environment they can enjoy?

Chapter 15   132

Becoming Conscious—
Outliers are curious, ambitious, authentic and often complex

Chapter 16   139

Accuracy of 'Feelings' is an Important Muscle to Grow—
Being aware enough to express your feelings

Chapter 17   146

Paradigm Shifts—
Through honest and sincere feedback comes a paradigm shift

Chapter 18   164

Collective Intelligence: The Futures—
Bringing potential into the world

References   187

Dedicating this book to the biggest influence in my life

It's 7pm on a Saturday evening in Toronto, Canada. I'm sitting in a small restaurant I have gotten to know all too well. The waiter knows my order by heart, my name, and why I'm there.

I'm with a small group of people, including my mother, Lois. Both of us are trying to find an appetite after a gruelling day.

All of a sudden, I get a strange feeling in my body and get up and start running back to the hospital room that has been our base camp for the past seven weeks. I get there just in time to be with my sister Jude as she dies in her bed. There are no words. Only tears as the others catch up a few minutes later to be with this 50-year-old woman whom we all love.

I stay for an hour or so, to be by her side for the last time. I know it's the last time I will see her face. So I stay. I stay. I reflect. I remember. I cry, like I am now. I stay. Of course time always runs out—in so many ways.

This book is dedicated to my sister who brought me up in the first seven years of my life. Taught me to laugh at the world when everything was going to pieces. Taught me to swear at the world when it felt right.

Most of all, she showed me what being tough in the face of adversity looked like, having seven hip replacements before melanoma took her down. You see, growing up in rural Aotearoa New Zealand meant she had missed out, by seven months, on having a routine examination that would have found she had a congenital hip disorder that could have been sorted as a baby.

Lots of sevens. Wonder what that's about.

She died in September 2000 at the Mount Sinai Hospital in Toronto. I miss her deeply. Always will.

 **Jude—thank you. This book is for you!**

Foreword

Harv had arranged for our first meeting to be in the coffee shop of a hardware store, which, as it turns out, sums him up pretty well on both counts. He was designed to bring people together to get stuff done. Two and a half hours into our one-hour meeting, I was hooked on the idea of Collective Intelligence.

In my experience, most organisations which claim to have a unique selling proposition are kidding themselves. Even the differentiated ones that have broken away from the peloton are usually just peddling a bit harder down the same well-worn track. Harv though, as you'll see, hasn't just taken the road less travelled, he's turned it into a fairground ride. He's a thought-leader who's more of a doer and has a 'lifelong dislike of leadership'.

He's a farmer who grows people. And he's a union rep for the planet, playing to a key strength of being a pain in the butt to heel-digging corporations and politicians alike. What makes him such a successful disruptor and challenger is that there's nothing he's keener to disrupt and challenge than himself. And that right there is the essence of Collective Intelligence.

Now, I've never heard Harv claim that this 'human ecosystem' he's created is unique, but he should because it is, and I should know because I've looked. Across both hemispheres, I've found everything from CEO networking forums to business process re-engineering consultancies to coaching programmes. And I've seen Collective Intelligence do all of that. But I've found no evidence of anything that replicates the curation of the teams, the intimacy of the investigations, the objectivity of the process, and the way the values superglue the whole approach together. Let alone the results.

That first meeting with Harv was perfect timing for me. I'd just stepped off a lifetime of climbing the corporate ladder, and was starting to re-invent myself—forging a niche helping leaders to become more adaptable. I was lifted by Harv's trademark relentless enthusiasm and curiosity about anything that might make a real difference. And I loved the novel idea of having access to a team of diverse and unbiased leaders who could offer the kind of perspective that would have taken me several lifetimes to gain on my own.

I was quickly welcomed into a team of immediately-impressive individuals who were at that level where they were such high achievers in their respective fields, they didn't need to impress anyone. So when it was my turn to ask for help, I felt both intimidated and completely safe at the same time. It was weird, but that's part of the magic of Collective Intelligence. I was intimidated enough to do the kind of homework my parents wished I'd done at school instead of playing drums in a rock band. And safe enough to ask my team to break the heart of my leadership model, knowing that it would be an ego-crushing step forward if they did.

Happily, they decided the model didn't need breaking, but there was a whiteboard's worth of feedback on how to improve everything around it. That included gold-dust advice on how to sell it, given by people who ran organisations selling everything from business consultancy to tractors. As a result, every time I now unveil the model to a prospect or client for the first time, my confidence is founded on the feedback my CQ team gave me that day, even though it's years ago now and 20,000 kilometres away.

A few years after that first meeting, Harv asked me to be the first guest on his podcast, 'Stuff That Matters Now'. This was back in 2019. Maybe it was because he knew I would have just stepped off a flight from London and would be the malleable guinea-pig he needed to help kick-off his latest big idea (now in its 6th season). But thankfully he decided to go easy on me. If leaders are defined in part not by the quality of the answers they give but the questions they ask, Harv should really re-think his dislike of leadership. Our conversation turned out to be serendipitous, because there we were talking about the need for leaders to be more adaptable given the increasingly unpredictable conditions, and less than six months later Covid shut down the world.

Long before *Clarkson's Farm* brought regenerative farming into the public spotlight, I remember touring the paddocks surrounding Harv's home one evening as the light was fading. There, with schoolboy enthusiasm he beckoned me to crouch with him and inspect the diversity of the pastures he was growing. Yes, even this man's grass has diversity! It's just another sign of his willingness and ability to challenge himself, which in this case involved nothing less than a handbrake turn on the entire way of unsustainable farming he'd grown up with. Monoculture does to nature what it does to leadership teams. They both look like well-proven models until the shit hits their brittle fans, exposing a catastrophic lack of resilience that was there all along. But that's not so easy to see or solve unless you make the effort to hang around with people who don't think, speak and act like you do.

By now you won't be surprised to learn that Harv lives by the mantra of 'go do what others won't and you'll succeed'. He's helped over a thousand people do things they wouldn't have done without the compass and cavalry that is Collective Intelligence. He stood up to lead not because he wanted the spotlight, but because he wanted to help. And that's a lesson that every leader everywhere should learn (and we're all leaders).

I reckon if you want to read a book about how to make the most of your life by challenging both yourself and others to make a difference, then read one written by someone prepared to do what others won't. Enjoy your first meeting with Harv.

Rich Alderton, High Performance Change

Introduction

If you've ever felt like you're the only one struggling to hold it together, then trust me, you're not.

I used to think that everyone else had it all figured out, and that I was the only one who seemed to not know what the big plan was. No one really knows what's going on. Not the person at the top of the corporate ladder, nor the influencer with millions of followers, nor the checkout operator at your local supermarket, and definitely not me.

But here's the thing: Real personal and collective growth happens when we own our imperfections, work together authentically, and challenge ourselves to break free from those old models of success.

So this is the book for anyone who needs to know that we're all just winging it. Anyone who's trying to make some sense of all the bullshit, and anyone who's ready to have a more honest conversation about what it means to live, to lead, to grow. That happens when we work together.

When we're interconnected, we can achieve things that no one's thought of. And when you bring people together to support each other, they end up growing themselves too.

The problem, as I see it, is that we know and care more about developing sports teams than we know or care about developing other professions. We've gone down the path of maximising profits, and that means plenty of other important ways we measure our lives—like happiness, sustainability, social impact, feeling alive and good about what we're achieving with our limited time on the planet—have been sacrificed.

We have ways of working that aren't sustainable, and are causing burnout and dissatisfaction with our lives, and a grim future ahead.

If you want a good metaphor for our future, then look to pine. We grow a lot of it in this country. It grows better here than in its native California. It's cheap and reliable for building and fuel, so we grow it in spades. But in the interests of efficiency, scale and profit, we've planted hundreds of thousands of acres of this crop as monocultures—literally the one species in repeating rows over huge blocks of land. It's easier to manage and harvest this way. And all the interdependents—the banks, the farmers, the fertiliser sales reps—want predictability, regularity, and consistent outputs. But a monoculture doesn't thrive or produce the best growth.

Nature wants diversity. Naturally-occurring forests are complex, with different flora, fauna and fungi finding their niche. The growth of ngahere (native forests) are unpredictable, but the long-term health is better, the growth richer, and the plants and soil thriving.

In monocultures, the plants still grow, but they lack strength. The wood is weak. It lacks resilience.

So I wasn't surprised, in the aftermath of Cyclone Gabrielle in early 2023, to see acres of plantations where the semi-mature pines had been snapped in half by the winds. The interests of rapid, straight growth had set the pines up to fail under the stress of a major weather event.

The nearby ngahere? Unaffected by the cyclone.

The current path we're on is the same as those pine plantations. And we know it. The gap between the rich and poor is growing. Oceania in particular, is going backwards when it comes to food security (i.e. knowing that we've got enough resources to keep us all well fed at all times). We're starting to see the loss of insect species—an early sign of ecosystem collapse. Habitats are degrading at an incredible rate. Water is becoming a scarce resource. Within the next 50 years, only the mega-privileged will have lives that are remotely enjoyable. We're in a worse situation systemically than we're prepared to admit.

We know that the old models of dominance and control, and power in a few people's hands, haven't worked. We have created solutions that benefit only a few.

That is, unless we do something about it now.

Living systems are complicated. They thrive off interconnectedness, and often off incredibly diverse species. To create different outcomes for the world, we need to look to nature for our business models and our lives and take a different approach to what 'success' means for all of us.

I founded Collective Intelligence in 2008. I had an idea: foster authentic growth and create a sense of belonging among our members. I wanted to see leaders developed, supported, and challenged by people from all kinds of industries, outlooks, and stages of life. And I wanted to draw on nature's principles to guide us.

In Collective Intelligence, we curate and create an environment for existing and emerging leaders, then facilitate better conversations and help those leaders grow in their confidence and abilities. We respond to what's in front of us. We're okay with uncertainty. We stay open. We keep our egos in check, too. And we're always learning.

We do it slowly, carefully, gently, by sharing stories that you wouldn't normally share. We cultivate a high degree of trust by demonstrating and creating spaces where people can be vulnerable (under the Chatham House Rule, of course).

And slowly, like a ngahere emerging from a one-farmed block of land, a resilient and dynamic new leadership appears.

I've had the immense privilege to work with over a thousand people across the years, and I wanted to share some of those learnings from my time, to help the next generation realise that behind every cool and successful person's façade is a lot of confusion, uncertainty and helplessness.

Because, as it turns out, no one's got their shit together.

But there's also a lot of hope. Life throws a lot of challenges at us. Not all of them come with powerful personal learnings or clever phrasings. But give it enough time, and you'll see a lot of it is interesting, and funny, and much better when you give it a go.

This is a messy book. You're going to read a messy story. It's not a self-help or motivational book. It's certainly not a business book. There are lots of learnings about self-help and motivation, and about business, but that's not where this book belongs. This is my story, and the learnings that have come with that.

Business books about personal development or personal stories tend to be a lot about maximising potential or building up an aura. Leadership events tend to be the same. Corporate people tend to follow corporate leaders. Farmers are in farmers' groups. We tend to want to dress up and follow the pictures of success in our fields. And that means there's a lot of ego, bragging, and loud voices. That's pretty expected. We want to learn how they became successful, after all, and copy that.

But all that'll ever give us is the status quo, over and over.

And we know that that's not good enough anymore.

We learn more from failures and in moments of vulnerability than we do during successes. We learn a lot from the quieter voices. People struggle. We don't grow well—let alone thrive—in a monoculture. We need diversity around us to grow strong, resilient, and healthy—in business, life, and everything around it—because it asks more of us.

And that takes time. I know it.

I've built each chapter in this book around my own experiences, and the real people and situations I've encountered along the way, in the hopes that it might shine a light on some of the parts of life that people don't really talk about. The story starts out with my early years in rural Aotearoa New Zealand, before looking at the unspoken secrets to good relationships and onwards to the founding of Collective Intelligence. From there, I talk about what real leadership looks like, and the glorious failures I've had as a professional. In the last third of the book, we cover some of the important lessons I've learned later in life: that vulnerability is where real growth happens, that diversity is the secret sauce to success, and finally, looking directly at the messy truth that no one has it all figured out.

My biggest hope for you reading this book is that you'll feel a bit more comfortable about the fact that life throws all kinds of weird shit at you. And you'll remember that you don't need to do it alone. No one's got it right, but we've got a better chance of figuring it out together. And the sooner we embrace that truth, the sooner we can start growing.

I would love to offer you a story of success, but what you'll find here is an invitation to think differently. It's time to let go of the old rules, face uncertainties, and grow alongside others in ways we never expected.

As it turns out, none of us know exactly what we're doing. But together, we can build something extraordinary.

Based on a true story.

Chapter 1

Influences are forever, even though the impact they have can be modified — Thankfully, it doesn't matter if you haven't got your shit together—yet

I was born in 1959, in the small rural village of Mangatainoka in the North Wairarapa. My family lived on a small farm situated on the banks of the beautiful Mangatainoka River, in a large wooden homestead built by my grandparents.

I can see now why it could be described as 'beautiful' or 'grand'. Old houses were like that. But they were also bloody iceboxes in the winter. Zero insulation will do that. So us three kids—me and my siblings Jude and Pip, both older—would run down the hall from the kitchen to bed with our hot water bottles clasped to our chests and jump into freezing sheets. It was bliss waking in the morning in a warm bed. Then we'd reenact the dash but back to the fire at the other end of the house, so we could keep our little bodies warm.

Mangatainoka had about 10 days of summer each year. The rest of the time was either rain or the threat of it. Our gauge was the Wharite Peak, our mountain that lies on the southern end of the Ruahine ranges. When Wharite had clouds halfway down the peak, it meant it was about to rain. If the peak was crystal clear, it meant rain was imminent. And if you couldn't see the peak, it was because it was already raining.

The upside was that my childhood was always green.

The big plus for me was the Mangatainoka river, teeming with brown trout and long finned eels. It was a constant source of fun for fishing, eeling and swimming when it was in a good mood, but when it was flooding, we all saw its darker side—a terrifying and damaging force of nature bringing down trees from upstream and ripping out fences and drowning livestock. This was before there were warning systems in place to notify farmers to shift stock to higher ground, and so families were often keeping an eye on the river—because it's all about the weather happening in the foothills of the Tararua Ranges that caused the flooding. My mother would lament that the river ruled her life.

Mangatainoka was a unique rural village: a mish-mash of unrelated and related industries that happened to be there for a variety of reasons meant there was a diverse makeup of families in the area. My guess is that the population in those days was around two hundred.

There was a local dairy factory where dairy farmers would bring their milk in vats mounted on trailers towed behind tractors, or on old Bedford trucks. These dairy factories were common across much of the country, and you can still see their old structures scattered across the landscape.

The dairy factory employed about twenty-five people, and some of their families lived in factory houses on its doorstep in order to start work around 4:30am to get the cheese starter culture going. This was a big deal, because if they couldn't get the culture to activate at this hour, it would cause havoc with the daily routine for everyone else. Culture starters were the kingpins.

There was one shop in our village, the General Store, which was a wonderful focal point for the community. You could buy just about everything you needed. This was before supermarkets came into being, so the trade that went on in these types of stores was brisk. You could get your mail, newspapers, vegetables, and socks all from one wee store. Plus gossip, at no extra cost.

There was also a railhead, where livestock and produce would be loaded off to the capital, Wellington, or to a regional centre of Palmerston North. Fertiliser and other large items were transported into the railway storage sheds.

The railway families lived in their own cluster of houses and were a tough crew. They lived and played next to the local pub, the Dudley Arms, which did a roaring trade. And like the General Store, it was a great source of gossip. If you wanted to know what was happening in town, this was the place to be. Even in my younger years, I became fascinated by watching my father, Bill, manoeuvre tricky conversations down at the Dudley from time to time. He was masterful at diffusing a volatile conversation, which I found fascinating and admirable.

There were the local dairy farming families, and a few sheep and beef farmers.

And then there was the brewery.

The Tui Brewery Tower

In our home, the view from my bedroom looked out at the river and a seven-storey brew tower some 500 metres away.

The North Island Brewery, which was merely a collection of small sheds, had been bought from receivers in 1903 by Henry Cowan, my great grandfather; my family were the majority shareholders.

There were a number of breweries (someone later told me there were at least seven) in the area for two reasons. First, because of the artesian water that had a unique taste. And secondly, the fact that the Wairarapa was 'dry', meaning busloads of chaps would venture up during a weekend to have a beer or two that they weren't allowed to have in their local towns.

Henry rebranded the brewery to the Tui Brewery in 1923 because of his love of the tūī birds that warbled on the kōwhai trees situated between the river and the Brewery. The Tui Brewery then was famous for its stout and its prize-winning East India Pale Ale which sold across the country. It had a rich history, and it was a very prosperous family business.

That tower—now an iconic landmark—had been commissioned to be built before the Great Depression began and was built by my grandfather Edgar Harvey in 1931. At that time, they could have easily been justified in halting the build due to the looming financial meltdown. Instead, they went ahead with it, costing £4,978 (New Zealand Pounds—about $515,000 in today's currency), and using local labour to keep the people in work. It remains a source of personal pride for me, not least because of the commitment it shows to the local community.

Because of the economic ravages of that time, they didn't utilise the tower for seven years after it was built. That and the fact it was an appalling design, making it near impossible to lug the malt to the sixth floor using a series of ladders. In 1938, a mechanical lift was added to the exterior, and the brew tower finally came to life.

I remember seeing how fast I could race up the ladders inside the tower, and I still have flashbacks of making it to the very top and peeking out of the wee windows. It was like being the king of the castle. The lift was a different story—it scared the hell out of me as it rattled and clanged on the way up, and you could see just how bloody high you were.

The diversity of people in Mangatainoka grew on the weekends as we had fishermen come from all around the world. The Toki River, as it was known, was famous for its trout flyfishing back in the day, and if you were a very good fisherman, you would catch four or five in a day. If you were an average fisher person you caught fuck all. But of course, they all thought they were good.

Looking back, I am very fortunate that our wee community had such a range of people, as diversity has become a cornerstone in my latter working life. It's hard to gauge just how much influence our community had on me. But it's significant.

Fishing the Mangatainoka

There were three people in particular who were important to the early years of my life. The first is my father.

My father Bill loved hosting the weekend fishermen. He'd tell them stories of what had been going on with the trout in the Toki during the week, teasing them with great tales of the river teeming with trout on a certain day.

(There are two fishing books written by Ted Webber and illustrated by Neville Lodge that he's been featured in, with wonderful—and accurate—regular sayings from Bill: *You Should Have Been Here Thursday* and *Come Again Friday*. If you should happen to see these books, I reckon his cartoon caricature is rather accurate too.)

My father would often come home during the week with some trout for dinner, and I could never work out how he caught them considering he didn't have a fishing rod. I was nine when he took me into his confidence, and we went fishing together—with his .22 calibre rifle!

It's bloody hard to shoot trout with a small calibre rifle, as you need to hit a target the size of a twenty-cent piece as the fish rises to the surface, so you can imagine the excitement for a nine-year-old, sitting up in a willow tree leaning out over the water, my old man waiting for the right moment, waiting, waiting for some trout to rise to catch a nymph. Finally, he got a clear shot of the trout's nose—the water going POP with the round, and the fish turning over. Then he gave me a wee nudge that sent me splashing into the river followed by instructions on where the trout was: I was to fetch the stunned trout. It was a total buzz.

One very memorable fisherman came down our dusty gravel road one beautiful Saturday in a big black car I had never seen the likes of before. He pulled up next to our old Morris Minor truck. His car was called a BMW, apparently.

Out jumps a very dapper fellow, puts out his hand to Bill to shake his, and says in a very posh voice something like "Brigadier General Thorton, Chief of Defence."

To which my old man replies in the same posh voice, "Bill Harvey, Farmer, Mangatainoka."

"I say, I hear there are plenty of brown trout in this river?" asks BGT.

"There are Brigadier, if you are able to catch them old chap."

I had never seen this play-acting before by Bill and was intrigued to know what was going on. It took a few years to learn that he didn't like snobs, Brigadier or not. However, it turned out BGT could fish and dropped in a couple of trout at the end of the day, having a Tui beer with Bill who then resorted to his normal voice.

Although I didn't realise it at the time, my father was highly unorthodox in most things he did.

His dress code was shorts and a black singlet, which protruded over his large belly (formed by drinking Tui by the Flagon). The singlet invariably had holes in the front with his hairy puku (a Māori term for belly) poking out. He would happily go to town dressed like this and talk to anyone he met.

He loved kids and was always concocting stories to tell them that were always unique as he made them up on the spot. My mother was the primary school teacher at Mangatainoka before they were married, and she was surprised one day when five of her students were very late for school. She was perplexed why all five were late and when she asked them why they said, "We've been waiting on the bridge over the Mangatainoka river for the big trout."

"What big trout?", asks the young teacher.

"There's a trout so big, it's got to go up to the bridge to turn around. We were waiting for it."

"Who told you this story?"

"Mr Harvey did! It's true. He was with us!"

And she still married him!

He also loved concocting stories for gullible adults. Never malicious, more opportunist.

One day when I was a kid, we were driving past the local dairy factory in his little white Morris Minor truck and he stopped to talk to the Manager of the factory. It was February and very dry. The Manager was a very earnest young man, and declared we were in the grip of a terrible drought (in Mangatainoka that meant about a week without rain).

"Yes" replied Bill, "you know the river has stopped running at the back of the farm". It was nearly too much for the manager to cope with, and he turned on his heels and disappeared back into the Factory. You see, the Manager drove over the river flowing freely on his way to work every morning!

Bill and I giggled all the way home—it kept us giggling for days.

The old man was reasonably liberal in his views of the world. My mother, not so much. One Saturday afternoon Lois had some church friends over, and they were voicing their displeasure on the latest streaking craze that was sweeping the country. It was disgusting behaviour apparently.

With that Bill gets up, takes off his clothes and walks down to get the mail. Came back, put his clothes on and declared, "it's not really that bad is it?" I remember the glare he got from my mother, and the deafening silence.

I think life had dealt him such a gruel blow with epilepsy that he would find joy and laughter in just about any situation. I loved that about him. He was a lot of fun to be around when I was younger.

This has rubbed off on me in many aspects of how I view the world—you've probably noticed a bit of this already.

I never did gain Bill's proficiency as a fisherman, though.

Life was idyllic living in this crazy mixed-up community with all its foibles and characters.

Mrs Peters

My mother Lois was a vital part of my upbringing, but she became sick with jaundice when I was born, so wasn't as prevalent as she could have been.

There were a number of options to help manage while she recuperated. The first was for baby Harv to be taken in by a large Māori family next door—and this was about to happen when Lois and Bill found a nanny.

So into my life came Mrs Peters, a Second World War survivor from the Balkans and a victim of the civil war that raged between the Croats and Serbs. Loud noises would send her sheltering under a table, and it would take some time to get her out. She apparently loved the Croat leader, Josip Broz—AKA 'Tito'—for his work trying to unify Yugoslavia after the war ended.

It was said that Mrs Peters was a very keen gardener of vegetables, and this was a great source of pride and comfort for her. She lived with her family on a street on the west side of a nearby town, Pahiatua. This street happened to be on the cattle stock route. Drovers would take cattle down that street from time to time.

The story that I remember most vividly was one in which one drover hadn't gone ahead and closed Mrs. Peters' street gate. This meant the cattle went into Mrs Peters property and her large veggie garden.

When she saw what was going on, she became enraged and went out the door screaming at the drover to get them out. He made the critical mistake of hurling some abuse back about her ethnicity, and suggested she should go back to where she came from.

My dad got a call a few hours later from the local Police in Pahiatua to say that they had Mrs Peters in a cell, and she was facing serious charges. The drover was now in hospital following the beating she had given him with a shovel!

When Bill got to the Police Station, there was Mrs Peters in the cell, still fuming. What he didn't understand immediately was that she was fuming not because she'd been arrested, but because the drover had been saved by a passerby who dragged her off—and so he had lived.

Bill gently tried to suggest she couldn't do that sort of thing—to which she scoffed at him and replied, "You have never been hungry. I kill him next time."

Time went by, and the charges were dropped after much discussion with the powers that be.

This had a huge impact on Bill, as he now had a whole new respect for the life she was carving out for her family in Aotearoa New Zealand. He found it hard to fathom the trauma Mrs Peters had been subjected to in her homeland.

Just in case you're wondering, no cattle ever got back into Mrs Peters' garden again. I'm sure the story to avoid Mrs Peters' place must have spread pretty rapidly amongst the droving teams.

In subsequent years, I've done some of my own research on the civil war that raged between the different factions all going on within the realms of the Second World War, and it's hair-raising reading the brutality dished out by both sides. I read that even the Nazis were terrified and felt unsafe at times even though they supposedly occupied the Balkans.

Jude

The other person who reared me in those first 1,000 days was my sister, Jude, ten years older than me. The bond I had with Jude was intense, and I can't imagine what my early life would have been without her influence. I idolised her.

The great irony is that we never spent much time together once she moved away for work in Wellington before I turned seven years of age, and then to Canada when I was 14 years old. But that never seemed to matter to our bond.

What has intrigued me was the combination of a Croatian refugee and the influence of my 10-year-old sister on my earliest development. Both of which have been the source of very positive memories.

It may sound harsh, but I am very grateful that this was the case, rather than my mother Lois' influence at that time.

The added bonus Jude brought into my life was her boyfriend and subsequent husband Tony Gaskin. I followed him around like a puppy. Tony has a wickedly sharp sense of humour and larger-than-life personality and provided a gateway into another world of commerce and marketing. Diversity, again, was broadening my view of the world.

I have another sister Pip, who is six years older than me and would become a huge influence on my development a little later. It was hard for Pip growing up due to the strength of the bond between Jude and me. She was also more sensitive than us, which we learnt more about as we got older.

All in all, this was a beautifully crafted childhood for a kid who likes people and the outdoors. I spent a huge amount of time eeling on the weekends or building elaborate huts from scraps of timber down by the river. These huts were strategically built near where the Girl Guides would come and camp on a weekend two or three times a year, until I reached puberty, and the Girl Guides were never to be seen again.

Nope, I don't want to talk about it.

Life at the Toki

50-odd kids (and to me some were indeed odd) attended Mangatainoka Primary school. Mangatainoka, as well as the river specifically, was called 'Toki' by the locals. Toki kids at the primary school were seen as sassy, naughty and tough. It was a real melting pot of cultures, backgrounds and social divide, and to us kids it was normal.

One day a new young Headmaster Jim Leogreen arrived. He was a clean-cut sort of fella, and sporty. Before his arrival, kids played mostly Bullrush and branding (like Bullrush, but between buildings in a confined space, we would throw a tennis ball to "brand" each other while we were running). These were high-energy, high-adrenaline games that could get you seriously hurt.

Jim, bless him, thought we were a bit feral, and that we needed to be "refined". His solution? Hockey was going to do it. No budget for the gear unfortunately, so instead we walked up the nearby Ruawhata hill to harvest some mānuka sticks out of the Papa bank on the side of the road. What a harvest we had. Jim was very impressed with our enthusiasm.

However, what followed was mayhem. We were told to take our sticks of mānuka home and work them into hockey sticks with the help of our parents. Now, the older girls fashioned their so-called hockey sticks into apparatus that could fell a twelve-year-old boy with a wee flick to his testicles no bother at all!

Poor Jim took a few weeks to get on top of the retaliations that followed. The sticks were all burnt, and we went back to Bullrush. Toki kids could be a tough bunch.

Life was idyllic, but I struggled at school.

One day, we were told that there were people here to test our hearing. I took little notice of this, until at the end of the day kids started yelling at me in a very comical way. What the hell was the joke?

I was to find out—after all the other kids had—that I had hearing loss. Up until that point I was considered a rather dull student with poor speech. Now I was deaf and dull.

It was easy to ignore the deafness and so that's what teachers did throughout my schooling.

I had got used to being left on the fringe of classroom activities because I didn't hear the instructions. It still happens now, if I don't ask for clarification. Try it—go put some earmuffs on and step into a crowded space. That's what it's like.

The hearing people told me that some jobs were now closed off to me. I would never be an airline pilot, for example. And all I thought was, *Sweet, I'm all good with that,* and went home.

My mother, however, was onto it in a flash, and informed me that she had organised for me to go to elocution lessons. My response? "No way am I doing that girly shit."

It was to no avail. Lois was not budging one little bit.

On a cold Monday afternoon at 3.30pm, I was introduced to my elocution teacher. Elizabeth Redman was a vivacious, eloquent red head. She also had a secret tattoo across her forehead that only I could see. It read, 'Do not fuck with me, boy'.

She was an amazingly tough taskmaster, and I lived in true fear of not completing my assignments on time. She entered me into *fucken* poetry competitions, and I remember reciting Beatrix *fucken* Potter in halls all over the lower North Island. The other kids were there to compete—I was there to get me on stage and just speak and to make sure I avoided Mrs Redman's secret tattoo!

Mrs Redman was tough, but she changed my life.

Elizabeth Redman was the first teacher who expected me to lift my game. She understood the hearing loss but treated it as just a barrier to be knocked down and learned to cope with. She would never accept my poor enunciation, and I found I would speak less and try to get the words right the first time.

Although she had students who did very well at the speech competitions, I was there just to get me up on stage. She treated me the same as them. I never felt inferior, and always challenged.

I had the great fortune and privilege of catching up with her a few years ago and had the opportunity to thank her profusely for the hours of tuition she put me through. It was incredibly emotional for me—her not so much. And yes, she still had that invisible tattoo on her forehead.

Despite the tattoo, she was the most positive thing I had in my life for a couple of years. And I needed it. Because around this time, life came crashing down.

Life happens when you least expect it

At Collective Intelligence, we often study the impact of early life experiences on people, their trauma, and sometimes we get a glimpse of intergenerational trauma and its impact. We have had the privilege to be exposed to over a thousand personal journeys. Due to this exposure,

I've come to understand just how impactful these journeys are on a person's trajectory and life.

I personally believe it's worth spending time to reflect and comprehend the key forces that have made a difference to mould us, all the while considering what has come before us. Māori have a wonderful term for this: *Whakapapa*. Te Ao Māori—the Māori language, and a respect and acknowledgement of Māori customs and protocols—has so many wonderful phrases from which we can learn so much.

So, when I reflect on my life, I look at the homestead and my family, the school, and how everything changed on the evening of 22nd of June 1970.

We were on a party line phone system. For those who've not heard of nor experienced a party-line system, it was one telephone line used by sometimes as many as ten households with everyone having a different number of 'rings' so you knew if the call was for your house. Our ring was *short-long-short*. Any other rings, you'd just ignore.

I was lying in bed when the phone went late one night. *Short-long-short.* My father picked it up. He was on the phone for what seemed like an eternity, and I could tell through the walls that the energy was being sucked from the air during the conversation.

I couldn't hear what was said, but I knew it was bad. I got up to investigate and he told me to go back to bed in a voice that I had not heard from him before.

When I woke in the morning, he was gone. My mother, white as a sheet, told me that something terrible had happened to my cousin Harvey Crewe and his wife Jeanette.

Harvey and Jeanette Crewe's house was found in disarray with blood-stained carpet, and their 18-month-old baby Rochelle left in her cot to fend for herself for five days.

I found out later that my parents had been concerned about Harvey and Jeanette for some time as there had been a number of instances of foul play over the previous 18 months or so. Their home had been broken into with personal items stolen, plus a hay shed had been set on fire. To top it off, the house had been set on fire when Harvey had gone to pick up Jannete and Rochelle from the maternity hospital. It seemed there was a personal grudge against them that was being enacted with a series of malicious acts.

My mother had received a letter from Jeanette 18 months prior saying all is well, and not to worry about them. The letter my mother received is chilling to me. The house fire had happened, and yet this young mother is replying to my mother saying all is well and not to worry about them.

Within 24 hours of that call, the case featured on the six o'clock TV news, and every newspaper and radio bulletin. It would be on the news every week for the next seven years.

The Police were dealing with a possible murder case, which in Aotearoa New Zealand at that stage was incredibly rare. For months, my father would be gone intermittently, as they searched for the missing bodies. The tension in the family rose as it appeared that Jeanette's father, Len Demler, was the prime suspect.

Harvey Crewe's sister Bev and her husband Don lived nearby to us, and they took custody of baby Rochelle. Within a week, we had Rochelle as part of the family. Harvey's mother, Marie, lived three miles away in the town of Pahiatua by herself. Our role soon became to be part of her support team, which as it turned out was to be 'on a hiding to nothing'.

Jeanette's body was found on 16th August 1970 in the Waikato River, and Harvey's a month later.

The investigation went into complete disarray. It appeared that the detective, Bruce Hutton, had been on the wrong trail pursuing Len Demler all that time. A team of detectives were then brought in from Christchurch to review the work of Detective Hutton's team. Unfortunately, Hutton's team had been in an echo chamber and dismissed key leads. As has been well documented by a Royal Commission of enquiry, Detective Bruce Hutton then set about framing a local farmer, Arthur Alan Thomas. This resulted in a successful conviction for the murders of Harvey and Jeanette Crewe.

There was a retrial, where Thomas was convicted again.

During that whole long process, my father would often claim that Thomas was never bright enough to commit the murders, shaking his head in disbelief at the conviction. In 1979, when it was discovered that

Thomas had been framed, he was pardoned and awarded $950,000 in compensation for his nine years in prison and loss of earnings. Bill's misgivings had been correct.

For me, this episode was an emphatic start to a whole different phase of life that saw me scrambling and struggling to come to terms with.

I saw the adults around me struggling to make sense of the world. It was like the adults had left the proverbial building.

My old man had always drunk a reasonable quantity of beer, but now he had taken to drinking whiskey or gin heavily each night, so that by dinner time he was morose, and would get up at the end of the meal and go to bed. Meanwhile Lois became depressed, and I would often find her crying by herself.

So, I put my head down. I didn't want to cause any bother. My role soon became one of supporting my parents, as both of my sisters had left home before and during this time. As an eleven-year-old, I found this challenging, to say the least.

My rock, Jude, lived three hours away, and I would see her when she would visit the farm with Tony for weekends. These visits were a source of huge joy for me. Jude and Tony would arrive back in Mangatainoka on a Friday night, having driven up in their new Nissan Violet from Wellington. It was like Christmas eve—but better. There was fun and laughter and Jude at 22 years-old, could lift her mother's mood whereas I couldn't.

Meanwhile Tony would head to the pub with Bill, and they would come back in a very jovial mood bringing a feed of fish and chips with them.

We would all muck around on the farm and look at my latest creation in the garden. Tony and Jude's friends would also call in and it was like a carnival compared to a regular weekend.

Leadership

It's at this point I developed a lifelong dislike of leadership. There were numerous moments in my early teens where I was helping to keep things together behind the scenes, and would think, *If I'm it today, we're fucked.*

I spent my school holidays from Rathkeale (my boarding school that you'll hear all about shortly) doing as much for both parents as I could in an attempt to bring some small glimmer of light to an otherwise bleak situation. It developed in me an unhealthy work ethic which has not been useful in my adult years. This looks like me jumping in when work needs doing, before thinking, *who should do the work?* Delegation is not something I do naturally.

I found myself having to make decisions that should have been made by my parents behind the scenes, leading to a very uncomfortable relationship by feeling responsible for outcomes that weren't suitable for a teenager.

Leadership just felt heavy to me.

This feeling is still alive in me today, even though I continue to work on it.

Meanwhile, my sister Pip had started at nursing college in Palmerston North, which made my parents very proud. Simultaneously, she started showing signs of bipolar disorder, although it took many years to diagnose accurately. In those days it was called 'having a breakdown', and all I knew was that her behaviour could become incredibly erratic, embarrassing and impossible to understand how to deal with for a young boy.

Trying to deal with her condition was one of the hardest things of all for me, because it was so intense and 'in your face'. It's still hard. God knows what it's like for her.

My father became morose at times and started drinking heavily during the week. My mother's depression deepened, although it was never talked about as such.

There was another wee sideshow during this time, where random adults—who knew I was Harvey's cousin—would like to take me aside and ask who committed the murders. It was quite apparent that the public were not at all certain that the police had caught the correct killer in Arthur Alan Thomas.

As a result, the golden rule imposed by the elders of the family was this: Do not talk to anyone about the murders—ever!

My memories of this time could be summed up in one word: *Alone.* I mastered a couple of things as a result: hiding my emotions and holding my breath under stress. I'm still trying to grow out of the second one.

Once I started withholding about the Crewe Murders and Pip's mental health, I started to withdraw from lots of conversations—scared I would blurt something out. I didn't feel like I fitted in anymore in Mangatainoka, nor Rathkeale. I spent my school holidays alone on the farm.

Even though I'm an extrovert, I withheld myself more and more. I have spent large chunks of my life being on the outer, and it's something I just accept at times, and at other times it feels a bit burdensome.

The irony of my work, mixing with such diversity in Collective Intelligence, is that I often attend functions where I only know one or two people out of hundreds, and this is normal for me.

High school

My two sisters had attended the local Tararua College, and I was destined to follow. But my sister Jude intervened and suggested that I needed to get out of the toxic environment that I was living in and be sent away to a boarding school. This was a complete and utter surprise to me, which I fought against, but once again with little effect. My maternal grandfather Willian Charles Deller was still alive at this point, and he was very keen for me to go to a particular boarding school in the Wairarapa called Rathkeale.

I had a very vague understanding of its existence. It was considered an elite school, and my grandfather was willing to help support my attending Rathkeale financially; my family were unable to afford the boarding school fees. My mother had recently gone back teaching at the local primary school, which was a godsend for her mental health, and ultimately meant that I could stay at Rathkeale.

The reason for our financial demise was a combination of factors, but mostly due to my father's poor health. It was an odd experience: living in this grand house built by my grandfather behind a brewery that had once created huge family wealth, living with elderly parents who were struggling to make ends meet and who sent their son away to a private boarding school.

But Jude was insistent and got her way.

One of the conditions of going to Rathkeale was that I was not to talk to anybody at the school about the Crewe murders. But this also meant that I would be sitting in a common room watching the 6 o'clock news with my mates, when my family would appear on the TV screen at a trial or retrial. Once again, it was incredibly lonely at times. It meant more holding of my breath and not showing my emotions.

The other difficulty was that this was essentially a decile 10 school, with boys from socioeconomic backgrounds that were vastly different from mine. Their holidays were filled with travel; mine were filled with working for my parents or fencing and joining shearing gangs to help pay for my school clothes. I was often envious, and sometimes jealous.

However, I was fortunate that I was a big kid and enjoyed physical labour.

When I was 14, both of my sisters chose to travel. Jude was married by this time to Tony Gaskin, and they decided to head to Canada for Tony to follow his marketing dream. The plan was to leave for three years. I was heartbroken. At the time, I didn't know that I would not see them again for seven years. They would never return to Aotearoa New Zealand to live.

Pip headed to London, travelling with a nurse that she had been working with at Palmerston North Hospital. Her bipolar condition still had not been accurately diagnosed, and as a result her medication was changing like her behaviour. She was erratic, to say the least.

Meanwhile, at school, I'd been told to sit up at the front of class because I'm deaf, and pay extra attention to the lesson.

Being deaf is no fun. People can't see it. You can't hear it. And the gap in between is huge. If you are deaf, and sit at the front, then you have no idea what is going on with the 30 other boys in the class.

That's dangerous. And no fun. You go ask a question that has just been asked—and answered—and see what reaction you get from a classroom of teenage boys.

So instead of sitting at the front, I sat in a back corner and perused the terrain from there. I developed a coping mechanism of creating havoc using humour, often at someone else's expense when I didn't know what was going on. It can be a very effective tool when it comes to levelling the playing field—especially if there are stronger boys in class.

The other thing that creeps into your subconscious when you are deaf is that you are dumb. Well, it did for me anyway. It's still a battle I have to fight from time to time. Even if there were experiences to the contrary.

I was fifteen, and I got the results back from a School Certificate mock English exam. There was a question worth eight percentage points. It was a Charlie Brown cartoon strip. You had to read it and answer some questions—notably, what the cartoon was about.

I had a very cool English teacher called Grant Harper, who was reading the scores out to our C Grade Class. They were mostly zeros or one or two points. This had played out in the A and B Grade Classes as well, as it happens. Mr Harper was reading out the scores from zero up. The highest score in our class was a three out of eight. He had missed my name out—or so I thought.

"Harvey, can you please let the class know what this comic strip was about?"

I thought I had fucked up, again.

"Well," I said, "I thought it was about..." and I went on to explain what I had interpreted from the cartoon. I can't remember now the exact words I used to describe the strip, but I would have talked about what it said about the relationships between the characters, and their personalities, and other things that you could make sense of out of the strip.

He looked at me and gave me this wonderful smile and said, "And that's why you got an eight out of eight for this section. Well done!" I found out later only two other boys in my year group got the same mark.

That was the one and only academic high for five years of high school, but it was something. A glimmer of intelligence had crept out from under the carpet. I feel very emotional just reflecting on that moment right now, because it gave me some pride—I had finally achieved something. Maybe I wasn't so dumb after all.

Keeping my head down

Rathkeale was a place for me to do as well as I could and have a rest from the shite at home.

That was until I got a call up from John Norman, the principal, to say they were making me a School Prefect at the beginning of my 6th form (Year 12, and a year early). This was apparently to prepare for bigger things the year after. The school was in growth mode, and there was a new boarding house being built; the House Masters' home was already in place. He wanted me to be the head of that Masters' house full of seven 5th formers.

How do you say no to that in the moment? All my defences were down, and I said my thanks to Mr Norman. So, at the beginning of my 6th form, I had a higher status than many of the 7th form boys, and I was thinking, *What the hell did I do to deserve this?* I was here to rest and hide!

My mother was so proud. Here's the picture I had in my head: Being in a senior leadership role the following year, and not being able to hear a question from a kid at assembly or being put in a position I could not hide from. I was not going to let that happen—so I got myself demoted. I had to try twice. The first action was seen as a blip on an otherwise clean slate. The next misdemeanour soon after was a sign they had made a mistake. Which they had. I was sure of it.

That voice in my head again was saying, *If you are in charge, Harv, we are in trouble.* The last year went as planned with me, all the while, being a very average student. Boom.

This leadership malarkey was not for me. I still struggle with it to this day.

Oh, and why didn't I go and get some hearing aids fitted you may think? It was 1977, and yes, hearing aids had been around for a while, but they made everything louder—not just the range you are missing. I tried them, and they were ghastly to wear. Frightening at times too, as the slightest noise would boom down your ears.

I found most sports easy. I held a school junior long jump record for 22 years, captained the school basketball team, and was in the rugby 1st XV, but tennis was the sport that I loved the most. In most sports you get coaching of some sort, and hearing and listening to the coach is kind of important, especially in a team sport. With my poor hearing that was an issue. But in tennis it was way more intimate—often being one-on-one.

I had learnt to play tennis at school and was ranked number one in our province of Wairarapa for the Under 18 grade. My tennis coach thought I should have a go at getting into a coaching clinic in Australia to train. I did, and to my great thrill was accepted at the Harry Hopman coaching school. At the time Harry Hopman was coach of the Australian Davis Cup team, so it was a big thrill to be accepted. My role was to be taught how to be a professional coach, not to become a professional player. I had only played tennis for five years, and never reached a national ranking.

However, before I could go off and do this, I had to settle the second condition of me going to Rathkeale set by my old man before I started. He stipulated I needed to work for six months at the Tui Brewery after I finished school.

His idea was to balance out what five years in a toff school might have done to me by seeing how the other half lived. I could still be accepted into the second intake of Hopman's coaching school in May, so all good.

Working in the jungle

What a shock to the system, though. I left school one week, and started in the bottling hall at the now modernised Tui Brewery the next.

120 blokes worked there at the time. Beer was on tap, and free from lunchtime onwards, so many alcoholics worked there (or became alcoholics working there). It was a fucken' jungle, with a definite pecking order. There were five schoolboys, taken on for the holidays that led up to the Christmas rush, and we were at the bottom.

We started packing pallets of cartoned dozens of beers from 7am through till 5pm. It was physically hard work, and boring as hell. I was used to shearing gangs where you had tallies to indicate how the day had gone. In this packing business, there were no tallies, and you had no idea if you had done a good day's work or not. You just stacked the pallets, wrapped them in plastic, and a forklift would take them away.

It was soulless work. Everything smelt of stale beer. There were no windows, since sunlight is not good for beer. The plant rattled to the hum of electric motors transporting tens of thousands of bottles a day. Returned empties were washed and sterilised, then put past Blue, a big fat Australian bastard, who was watching for tampons and used condoms that might be still in the bottles after washing. Blue sat on his throne every day for years doing his job of pulling out one or two bottles a day. It was unbelievable to a boy like me.

Bottles were then filled, pasteurised, and sent through to the waiting empty crates to be filled—12 bottles at a time—then on to us, the stackers. The noise of bottles clinking into each other was deafening, with people shouting at each other, or better still using an arrangement of hand signals.

The constant clanking of the bottles was possibly the first time that my hearing loss had put me on the same level as everyone else. No one could hear very well, hence the sign language, some of which was very colourful and detailed.

As the horn went for lunch, we'd all venture into the smoko room with up to 100 others at any one time. Older workers would yell at us to get them a beer—something I learnt to do as quickly as possible so as not to draw any undue attention.

The kings of the joint were the Engineers—described by others as "complete c**ts, and mean with it." I would quickly learn why.

I had a cousin, Paul Harvey, working alongside me, and we were singled out because of the association with our family founding the brewery. Paul was an athlete, with talent in shotput and discus, and as a sprinter—so he could move. He was built like an ox, too—a bit like his grandfather, Burt, who had been lugging kegs around the brewery sixty years prior.

Paul got singled out one random afternoon by a couple of brothers in their late twenties who thought they would put him in the shower for fun. We schoolboys tagged along to watch for a laugh, as these two white trash brothers jostled him into the shower block.

Do you know the sound that scalding hot water sounds like when it's pouring onto the ground? Well, the shower was making that sound, with steam billowing from the shower cubicle, from water delivered directly from an industrial boiler. It would have taken skin off, it was so hot.

Paul saw what was intended for him and went nuts. We ended up having to save the brothers from real harm within about 60 seconds, as Paul was in a complete rage throwing these poor buggers about. Blood spread all over the floor and wash basins. These poor buggers were concussed, bruised, with cuts all over their faces. I thought we were in big trouble.

But no—it was the law of the jungle. The janitor cleaned up the blood like nothing had happened. The white trash brothers took the rest of the week off work, hiding their scars. But word had gotten out.

We slowly learned why he'd been singled out. First of all, the boiling water—that had been set up by the Engineers. A few days prior, there had been a breakdown in the main bottling plant. It was all second-hand gear and prone to failure. Schoolboy Harv was sent off to find the Engineers at 3pm. I couldn't find them anywhere, until I was sent to the first floor of the Tower, and there they were playing cards with a tea pot full of beer.

I didn't get back until 3.45pm, welcomed by jeers of "Where have you been, schoolboy? Having a wank?" The plant was finally running soon after 4pm, meaning we didn't finish until 6pm. We filed into the cafeteria soon after for a beer, and an Engineer shouted to me, "Get me a beer, boy." I was tired and humiliated already, and responded in a very ungracious way. No need to write it down.

As it turns out, the white trash brothers owed the Engineers and were instructed to put "that Harvey ponce boy" in the shower that they would connect to the boiler to serve him a lesson. Unfortunately for them, they'd mistakenly picked the wrong Harvey!

After the shower incident, we never received any more shit. It got out very quickly that this bunch of schoolboys had earned their stripes.

The other half

My time at the bottling factory was a hell of a wakeup call after five years at a private school.

We were paid on a Thursday afternoon in cash, which was put into little brown paper envelopes and hand-delivered to us all by the accounts staff. I would see family men then take those envelopes into the smoko room and use the cash to gamble while playing the card game Euchre. It seemed once they got onto a losing streak they just couldn't stop. I would think about their families at home, waiting on that cash to buy food and clothes, and what it must have been like for the wives and partners at home waiting for their old man.

What an eye-opener.

Because I had been to primary school with some of these father's kids, now I had a glimpse into the reality of what they lived with. I had thought I was the only one battling with trauma at home.

This was the experience I realised my own father wanted me to witness up close. It was definitely impacting my view of a wider society. More lessons were to come.

It's so easy not to see how others live until you've been exposed to it.

It's so easy to be judgy of "those people" over there. The "others" who have a different way of life. Those who are closer to the bread line and often get punished more for it by politicians. It was evident to me even then that these people were products of a system that wanted to keep them in their place of low-to-medium wage labour. They would keep doing the work not many would choose to do, and often not have much choice about it, either.

It was the first time I felt my privilege seeping from my skin—even though I could not have articulated that back then.

I never wanted to do the full six months. I would have preferred the six-week stint the other schoolboys did. However, that enforced extra time made all the difference between a quick peep into this other life, and a deeper immersion in the kind of life so many people live. I didn't fully appreciate at the time just how important that was for my development.

In the meantime, Pip was engaged to be married in the UK to a chap she had met over there. Bill and Lois were going to travel over for the wedding. And I was about to head to Australia for my tennis coaching. Timing was tight, but it was all going to work out.

With the excitement of the impending wedding, Pip unfortunately entered a manic stage and decided to hop on a plane back to Aotearoa New Zealand before she became too ill. When she arrived, she was in a full manic state, which is what we encountered at the airport. So began a truly terrifying few days that felt much longer.

For those who have not experienced a manic person it's kind of hard to explain. Firstly they don't need sleep and can go for days without it. They become superhuman strong, and their filters for acceptable social behaviour just aren't there.

As Pip arrived at Palmerston North Airport (I hadn't seen her for four years) she took one look at me and hurled abuse at me at the top of her lungs. I had no idea what to do as everyone looked in my direction to see what I had done to receive this abuse. So I just walked out to the carpark and waited. It was a very long trip home.

The next morning I was sitting in the smoko room of the brewery with 100 other chaps and a roar went up. They are looking out the window and I follow their gaze. To my horror it's Pip dancing around the paddock just beyond the smoko room, with very little clothing on. *Oh fuck.*

The head fella Doug (a neighbour of ours) comes up to me and says, 'is that Pip?".

I said, "yep".

"Best you get her home eh."

As I went out through the glass door, the men went nuts chanting and carrying on, then suddenly went quiet—Doug had raised his voice.

I found Pip and said, "can we go home?". Luckily, she said "yes". Those next few days didn't improve much, until finally she was committed to a psych unit in Palmerston North.

Long story short, Pip's health slowly came right, and she ended up getting married here in Aotearoa New Zealand to her fiancée from the UK.

This took a big toll on an ageing Lois and Bill, and I realised I needed to support them as much as possible. I cancelled the Harry Hopman autumn intake for 1978. My parents asked if I could look after the farm for six weeks so they could go to see Jude in Toronto. Of course, I said yes.

When they got back, I had found a shepherding job in Taihape.

Fast forward to 2023—I bumped into my old mixed doubles partner Janey Field from school days. We were the respective singles and mixed doubles Under 18 champions for Wairarapa. We had both been accepted into the tennis academy in Sydney at the same time. I hadn't seen Janey or heard from her in 45 years. Her first words were, "Where the hell did you get to?" Of course, there was no social media or texting back in the late 1970s—I had just not turned up. She'd gone on to play tennis around the world.

I went home that night and felt utter resentment for not having gone to Sydney. It was a very bleak 24 hours as I pondered what Janey had experienced and what I had missed out on. I was feeling sorry for myself. Then as always, the fog lifted, and I thought of all the things that I had experienced that I otherwise would not have done. I wouldn't be writing this book for a start.

It's something I have learnt and re learnt. Comparing yourself to others is a race to the bottom. Yet it still creeps in when I'm not looking. So, I need to keep reminding myself that it doesn't really matter if you 'haven't got your shit together, yet'.

Reflections:

- What have been the influences and influencers that have impacted your development over the years?

- Which of those do you believe has had a major impact? Why?

Chapter 2

Why Authenticity Has Always Been a Fascination for Me—Authenticity: The unspoken secret of good relationships

It was the end-of-year prizegiving. I was in my 6th form year (Year 12) at secondary school, and all the parents are filing into their seats, shaking the hands of John Norman the headmaster and his wife Fay en route. It was all a bit tense, being the last event of the year and very formal.

John Norman was the founder of the school. He was very 'old school', and an imposing man. The boys' nickname for him was 'Jack'—but goodness, no one ever called him that to his face.

There I was, standing in line with my mates in my year waiting for the last of the parents to come through the assembly room doors.

Then my mate Gordon whispered, "Here he comes." He was referring to my old man Bill, who of course was with my very prim and proper mother Lois.

Bill spots the group of us in line. A big smile creases his face from ear to ear and he waves out with a "G'day, you boys," that cuts across the whole room—because no one else was talking, were they!

It got worse. Bill stepped up to John Norman, shook his hand, forgot his real name and called him "Jack." Then he kissed Fay on the cheek with a "Still love me?" comment (one that he often used with his many female friends) and proceeded to sit down and switch off for the entire prizegiving.

My mates just thought it was the most hilarious combination of events—one of the kind that had often played out in one form or another over the previous four years they'd got to see and know him.

He wasn't showing off. He really enjoyed my friends. He thought the school was okay as far as toff schools go (it wasn't his choice of colleges). However, he liked John Norman, thoroughly enjoyed Fay, and wasn't remotely interested in any form of academia.

To me he was being himself. His authentic self.

He had a wide range of friends and acquaintances and seemed to treat them all the same. These included a US Ambassador, who often came fishing on the Mangatainoka River and became lifelong friends with my parents going to stay with him in Hawaii many years later.

I remember one occasion in 1967, when Bill was called upon to host Lord Moyne, who was visiting from the Guinness brewery in Ireland: our local Tui Brewery was then brewing Guinness beers. The local brewers were in awe of this brewing royalty coming to visit and wondered how they were going to entertain Lord Moyne. They soon hit on the idea of utilising Bill as unofficial host.

As it turned out, it worked a treat. Bill soon learned that Moyne was an author of children's books, so took him off to the local kindergarten run by Bill's sister, Marie. Moyne and Bill had a great time playing and talking with the kids. This was totally off-script and caused a bit of a dilemma for the organisers.

The only glitch in the few days he hosted Lord Moyne was a bit of friction between my old man and one of Moyne's travelling footmen. Bill found the footman a bit stuffy and a snob. Being a snob was one of the worst things a person could be, in Bill's eyes. He would smile and say, "They've got tickets on themselves."

The footman definitely had tickets on himself—apparently.

Bill wasn't much of a church goer and didn't class himself a Christian. He was more interested in just helping people. I had many discussions with Lois about the merits of Christianity versus what Bill practised. These got a bit heated from time to time.

So it's a curious thing that he developed a very strong bond with our local Archdeacon of the time, Doug Weaver. Doug would turn up occasionally on a Friday afternoon to sit with Bill at our kitchen table to chew the fat. Lois would go into a spin, and get very excited Doug was there, only to be scolded by Bill to leave the poor bugger alone. "He's been with you bloody Christians all week," he'd say. "Now give him a break."

The kitchen was off limits until the conversation between Doug and Bill was finished. Then Doug would quietly slip out the door to head home. I would come in to see Bill very quiet and contemplative. He would often remark, "You know Harv, that's a bloody tough job Doug's got."

What stood out for me being around my father is that he was always interested in the person, more than what they did or their title.

My Father—Authenticity

As I matured and learnt more about my father, I became more fascinated about what he stood for, and the freedom he gave himself to live his life. He had many personal setbacks as an epileptic (a thing of shame to hide from people in those days), was an asthmatic, and had some poor learning skills—and yet he woke most days with a smile on his face and was happy to be alive.

From time to time he would recall the early days of the Second World War breaking out and how he tried to enlist in the New Zealand army, but to no avail as he was an epileptic. He was 19, and so joined the Home Guard. That really sucked for Bill. Some locals took it upon themselves to post white feathers to him in the mail, thinking he was a coward for not enlisting. He would have tears rolling down his face as he told me about this, as he felt totally powerless to respond in any way.

At his funeral, his old mate Doug Weaver gave a wonderful eulogy, and for the first time in public talked about the white feathers being sent, and the impact it had on Bill. You could have heard a pin drop in that church. It felt wonderful to finally have that out in the open. People came up after the service in tears saying how sorry they were—I never had the guts to ask for which part they were sorry about. I was wrung out.

I'm wrung out now writing this. Time for a break.

It takes time to unravel what impact key people in your lives have on your development, as it's often subtle and hard to get a grip on. I do know I was very lucky to have this man as a father.

My prim and proper mother Lois couldn't have been more different. We three kids used to muse why they ever got married in the first place, conceived three children (Bill went to bed and rose early, and Lois was the complete opposite), and parented together in such different ways.

Lois was a primary school teacher who arrived in Pahiatua to teach the Polish refugee children at the camp after the Second World War. She was a history buff, a debilitating perfectionist, a church goer and an academic.

Her birth mother died when she was seven years old, and in those days, children were seen and not heard. She didn't quite know what had happened to her mother, until her father remarried soon after and she found she had a new mother.

I know this sequence of events left an indelible stamp on my mother for the rest of her life. I often wished she had been able to access professional counselling to help her with her depression, procrastination and need for perfection, but alas her generation didn't have that sort of help available. I'm not sure she would have used it even if it was available.

Her father, my grandfather, William Charles, was a stuffy old bugger who loved breeding horses, and was a bit of a snob. He didn't approve of my father one little bit—not that Bill could give a flying monkey's.

So I had these two parents, Lois and Bill, who came from totally different backgrounds and set of values and interests, who were a constant source of wonder and amusement to me. I don't think today they would have stayed together. I'm sure my mother would not have had children, and instead focussed on her academic career.

I was very close to my old man, and we would spend weeks together on school holidays. It was always fun and interesting, as he loved people and we would go seek them out for a chat. Work on the farm was something to fit around socialising during the day.

Meeting my Mother

My mother worked most of the time, in one capacity or another. She would beaver away on a wide range of chores like ironing hankies and washing plastic bags to reuse. Both grew up in the depression, but it seems it had a way bigger effect on Lois. This makes sense as the family's financial situation was vastly different than through that earlier period.

However, the biggest difference between the two was that Bill was happy in his own skin, lived in the moment, treated everyone as he found them, and had freedom to go about his life being himself.

My mother, on the other hand, always seemed to be trying to be something unattainable most days. In my teenage years I spent most school holidays working on landscaping projects around the home (which I thoroughly enjoyed) that I thought would help her to find happiness. Of course her happiness never seemed to last. It's very sad for me to reflect on this now.

The biggest learning I had with Lois was when she was diagnosed with terminal cancer when she was in her mid-80s. She was given around six months to live and received the news with a great positive energy. It was as if she decided that she needed to make the most of the time she had left.

She was in little or no pain, minimum medication, and her brain was as sharp as ever. What a six-months we had together! She changed so much from the mother I had been used to. I was shocked at times by the open conversations we had and would check with the head nurse if this was anything to do with her state. The nurse knew her well; they were part of the same church. She'd smile at me and say, "Nope—you are meeting someone who was always hiding behind the facade she had created."

This culminated one morning as I was reading her the Dominion Post—a ritual we tried to do every morning. She was propped up in bed, and I read from the chair next to her. There was an article about the USA, and she was chuckling to herself about the fall of the American empire which she had been marking down for the past 10 years. This particular article was another example to her of the sheer pace of that fall.

There was reference to the Second World War in the article, and I asked her about the war years for her. Her response is now part of the family lore.

She said it was very exciting, and a lot of fun for many of us at Teachers College. "We were not supposed to say that, but in reality, it was the most exciting thing to have happened to us in our lives especially with the American soldiers stationed at nearby Trentham camp. They had lots of money and were very attentive," she explained.

"The war was happening a long way overseas in a different world, and while we were very aware of the plight of the young men and women serving in the army, back home it was pretty cool." She went on. "You had to be very careful—because, of course, there wasn't contraception in those days."

Lois and I had had many conversations about contraception and its effect on behaviour of youngsters nowadays prior to this revelation, but up until now there were never any personal stories from Lois about her own experiences.

Now, here's where I made my mistake: I asked about her good friend Betty who was at Teachers College with her and was a bit of a hard case. I asked if Betty was a bit naughty with the American soldiers. Lois smiled, and said, "No not at all, as she had met Bruce her fiancée at this point and was very loyal to Bruce." All good—or so I thought.

Then she fixes me with her gaze from 1.5 metres away (I know, I measured it later), and proclaims that, "Betty never really liked Bruce ejaculating inside her, even when she was happily married."

What the? *Okay it couldn't get worse*, I thought.

She goes on to say that she didn't think Betty had ever had an orgasm, poor woman. Then proceeds to tell me (not for the first time) that Bill was a great lover (due to his French genes apparently), and she had had lots of orgasms.

I'm dying—1.5 meters away!

Then she levels a very direct question at me, "Do you think women should have orgasms?"

I was about to say, "I didn't know they could, Mother," when a nurse came in, and I fled that room as fast as I could.

The Head Nurse came over to check on me as I was scarlet. I relayed the conversation. She was in hysterics.

"What the hell is going on?" I asked.

The nurse just said, "Harv, meet your mother."

Lois died peacefully about three weeks later, and I had the privilege of giving the eulogy. There is no greater honour.

"While I would miss Lois," I said, "I needed a break from the last six months." I relayed some of the stories (not this orgasm one, obviously) from the past six months and how I had been introduced to my real mother.

During the eulogy, I reflected on the terrible loss of not being able to meet her fully earlier in life. It was joyful and yet deeply sad. As I sat down, there was an ovation for the eulogy. I felt very content at that moment.

After the service the head nurse came up to me and said, "Harv, Lois would have been very proud of you delivering that eulogy."

I shook my head. "No she wouldn't. It wasn't perfect."

"Well, I know the mother you had for the last six months would have." She was right.

These are some of the influences that burn in my heart, as to why authenticity is just so important to me each and every day.

Reflections:

- What impact does authenticity play in your day-to-day life?

- Who would you say is the most authentic person you've known?

Chapter 3

From Shepherd to Uni Student — Go do what others won't do and you'll succeed

In the mid spring of 1978, I was on my way to a new life chapter. I was driving my beige Vauxhall van (chick magnet for sure) with my wall-eyed heading (sheep-herding) dog 'Pete', to a place called Mataroa situated on the northwest side of Taihape.

I felt a fair bit anxious, because the fella who I was to work for thought I knew more about farming than I really did. Yes, I had grown up on a farm. And yes, I had been looking after our small farm while my parents were away for three months (with some guidance). But in reality, I knew sweet fuck all.

My first day I was helping out with the docking. Pete got very excited as we penned this mob and bit me on the arse, and the fucker wouldn't let go. It's jolly hard pretending it doesn't hurt in front of the new team, when it hurt so much—in fact I had a monster blue and black bruise on my bum for quite a while.

So, apart from a sore arse, I was free with clear air ahead of me. What a magical 18 months it was! Meeting new friends, my future wife, and falling in love with this beautiful place. Taihape soils are some of the best you will find on any hill country in Aotearoa New Zealand. They are papa-rock based (a soft, blue-grey mudstone), with a volcanic overlay, and livestock thrive on this soil.

However, it's no place for below-average farmers, with very long cold winters, and hills for as far as the eye can see. This provided an environment which was wonderful for a young shepherd to learn his trade. Farm here, and you can farm anywhere.

By North Island standards, it's a bit remote, which meant the local community needed to create its own fun and entertainment. And did they ever!

Learning can be fun

However, the greatest impact on my personal development during this time came from an unexpected source. During my Rathkeale school days, I had developed an unlikely friendship with a boy from Taupō, Michael Herbert. Michael and I were like chalk and cheese, but we got on very well.

As it happened, his father Ross Herbert used to know my great uncle Burt Harvey from the Tui Brewery days. Michael sought me out and invited me to stay with them, which I did from time to time. It was wonderful staying with the Herberts, because I got to experience a happy functioning family, which was an absolute tonic. Staying with the Herbert family was the best time I had during my teenage years.

Ross Herbert, who was originally from a farming family in Herbertville, was now farming north of Lake Taupō near Kinloch. It was a small farm he had drawn in a Government Ballot system that aimed to assist people to start a new career in farming. This often meant they were able to settle what would be deemed otherwise marginal land. It was an innovative system which was sometimes wonderfully successful, and sometimes not, depending on the block of land and the ability of the young farmers who drew the ballot.

The Herberts drew a poor piece of land, but they were clever buggers. Dorothy Herbert was also from a farming family and would run the farm while Ross would find casual work on the surrounding state-owned Landcorp Farming Limited blocks. They were excellent stockmen and women, and Ross was a talented welder and could put his hand to anything.

The whole family were into waterskiing, and Michael and his brother Paul were into barefoot waterskiing by the age of 10. The Herbert family worked hard to play hard. To me it felt like an oasis as it was so different and refreshing compared to my troubled family experiences at that time.

Ross was also a National Dog Trial champion, and even though he had now finished competing, that skill remained.

The Herberts lived only two hours from where I worked in Taihape, and many weekends I'd pack up and head to Kinloch, taking my dogs with me. By now, Pete had two mates and had learnt not to bite me when he got excited!

What an amazing opportunity to be able to learn from a master stockman with one-on-one lessons that happened during the 18 months I was based in Taihape. The gift my father had allowed by encouraging me to look at other professions was paying off. As a result I didn't have to unlearn bad habits. Unlearning is hard.

On these weekends, I would arrive on a Friday night and sit down with Ross at their dining room table, and unload stuff that was frustrating me with the job, or things I needed help with. To say I was infatuated with this wise and generous man is not far from the truth. He had this drawl while speaking which I would try and copy when he wasn't about.

But he made me think like nobody had made me think before. He would tease me at times and make me argue a point. Every now and then he would shake his head and say, "Argh… Harv, you are dumber than I thought," at which Dorothy would jump to my defence. Ross would just shrug his shoulders and go to bed. So much growth in such a short space of time—I'm glowing inside as I write this now, as it was the first time I had found learning fun.

Some of my most important learnings

Here's the lessons from Ross that stuck with me most.

I asked him one day why he didn't still compete at dog trials (age is no barrier to competing). He told me, "I've done that, and now it's time to learn something else to keep me young." He went on to say, "It's not good for you to just keep on doing the same things, but instead start again with something new."

As well as teaching me to think, Ross was also learning the art of lapidary. This meant collecting interesting rocks while on holiday with the family, taking them home, and cutting and polishing these into items that could be sold into the growing tourist trade of nearby Rotorua. The funds from this went into the boat and fuel needed for water skiing. Smart eh! A learning for me that showed up in my 30's when I later started sculpting.

Another thing I learnt from Ross was how to manage my frustration with my boss, Bob. Now, Bob, who was a great chap despite my frustrations, had a shite pack of dogs who were not well trained. When we were mustering ewes and lambs in particular, the job was often really hard work—hence my feelings of frustration that I knew I really couldn't discuss with Bob.

When I told Ross about this, he smiled and said, "Get up earlier and do it by yourself."

I replied, "Why? We already have 5am starts."

"Well," he said, "get going at 4am—go do what others won't, and you will succeed."

So that's what I did, with Bob now turning up as I was completing the muster. It wasn't that subtle, but it was a hell of a lot less work and far more enjoyable.

"Go do what others won't"—has stuck with me and shows up in many ways till this day.

To Ross and Dorothy Herbert—thank you for showing me how to have fun, work hard, and keep learning—I wish you were alive to read this tribute.

What a wonderful period in my life, surrounded by newly-made friends, beautiful scenery, and a dog Pete who didn't bite me anymore. Most weekends our core group of mates would get together on a Friday night and just make fun shit happen.

The power of the sub-conscious

One such moment near the end of my time in Taihape, my mates and their girlfriends had gathered one evening on the banks of the Hautapu river and were trying to find some music on a car radio. It was 7pm and the first news item came on. It was December 17th 1979, and a Royal Commission of Inquiry had been looking into the police conduct during the Crewe Murder investigation. The news item said that Arthur Allan Thomas had been released and pardoned of the murders. He would be granted $950,000 in compensation.

I froze when I heard the news. Held my breath. Showed no emotion. I didn't know how to process this and wandered off by myself. To the other 17- to 19-year-olds with me, it wasn't even newsworthy.

This single event had more impact on me than anything else, even if I didn't know it then. Inside I was stewing. I couldn't talk to Jude because she was in Toronto. I couldn't find a release. It would come, but later.

The tyranny of untamed humour

After 12 months of shepherding, I decided to go to Lincoln University just out of Christchurch to complete a Diploma of Agriculture. I chose Lincoln to get away from home base and stretch my otherwise narrow experience of the world.

I found myself at Lincoln two months after the news of Thomas's release, still stewing but not actually knowing what had got under my skin. It's taken years to work out the impact of this trauma.

An involuntary release came about two months into my time at Lincoln, and totally caught me off guard. Such is the power of the subconscious.

Back then it was as cheap as chips to go to most universities. Tuition was basically free—you just needed to pay for your board and tucker (and beer, of course). Doing the rounds of the universities in 1980 was the Aotearoa New Zealand United Students Association, led by a charismatic President in Simon Wilson. I think in time he may have gone on to a career in politics.

Simon was on a mission to raise the financial support from the Government for students with a new initiative called a 'hardship grant'. It's fair to say, us 'Dippies' (as we were called) had little need of such a grant, having worked for two full years before we got to Lincoln. But a few of us thought we would go along for a listen to the esteemed Simon Wilson of the NZUSA. Simon was compelling and was definitely on a roll with his mission. I was listening sort of intently, until Simon said in a very convincing tone, "You and I are the elite youth of the country and need the financial support to develop our superior skills."

My reaction took me more by surprise than anyone else.

I jumped up. "Excuse me?"

"Yes?" says Simon.

"I think you have the wrong room here, mate. Let me check." I shouted out to the few hundred students: "Could the elite youth of New Zealand please stand up." A couple of plonkers did—bless them.

"Thought so, Simon—you are in the wrong place." And I walked out to howls of laughter and a hundred or so students followed.

Well fuck did I get told off by the Lincoln Students Association! "How dare you make a mockery of the NZUSA president," they said.

Fair call. "But he's a twat for saying we are the elite youth of New Zealand." And that's where it ended. For that episode anyway.

This behaviour of mine continued into lectures and field trips to the point where I got called into the Dean's office mid-year to hear, "Mr. Harvey, pull your head in or you are out."

Lincoln was a very tolerant place, so I had obviously gone just a bit too far.

I'm relaying this as it was a major hurdle for me to overcome. I felt as if I couldn't control this rage against something that was invisible to me. The other students thought it was great fun to hang out with this chap Harv that could go off in broad daylight (and sober at that) at an esteemed professor—the best fun ever which led again to the Dean's office.

Finding the growth of personal joy

However, it didn't go away when I left Lincoln and would show up from time to time. After years of counselling and self-reflection, it started to make sense.

And here's why.

Back to the Royal Commission of Inquiry. When Thomas was released, the Commission found that the police had planted evidence to convict him, and something inside of me processed this as: *You fucken adults have been covering your arses instead of doing your high-profile jobs.*

The result is that you have destroyed lives.

I began to judge anyone I thought was not being responsible in the roles they held. Now, it can get messy doing this, and it did from time to time. Being self-righteous feels so good. This was the first step of my unlearning journey.

However, there was a silver lining to my trauma of the Crewe Murders. With the help of Professor of Practice, Michael Philpott (who has experienced trauma in his life too), I later uncovered my key personal driver of keeping Collective Intelligence going, and that brings me great joy.

For my family, the murders were tragic and traumatic. However, what was even more harmful, I believe, was the misinformation that was created by the corruption and mishandling of the case by the authorities.

None of this must have been much fun either to the police and officials, who were doing the best they could, with the tools they had, under the immense pressure, and in an echo chamber.

Now what keeps my fire burning with Collective Intelligence is the joy I get when our members gain unbiased, clear information they can take forward in their lives, so they can take action with the wisdom created by their Collective Intelligence teammates. This can never be underestimated. It's priceless.

If my family and others had been able to access unbiased clean information they could trust, our lives would have been far different.

The irony of all this reflection and story is that Collective Intelligence has been driven by trauma and pain, and reflection, and more pain. For me it's not the trauma that I want my life to be determined by, but rather the response to the trauma. It's work in progress every day.

Reflections:

- What have been some of your most important learnings?

- What brings you personal joy? How do you access and nurture this joy?

Chapter 4

The Rag Trade is Bloody Tough —
When authenticity is all you have in the tool kit

"Yeah, is Steve Oh there, please?"

"No, Steve Oh is not here. Who is this please?"

"Ian Harvey. Who is this?"

"This is Interpol. We would like a chat please, Ian. See you tomorrow at 3pm in Auckland."

That's never a good way to start the day!

How did I get here? Well this will take a bit of unravelling.

The cashmere fibre is regarded as the most luxurious of all the natural fibres in the world and has been coveted for centuries. It was originally produced from Kashmir in India and later was a symbol of wealth in Europe.

It's grown by many different breeds of goat and is a secondary follicle hair that is super fine in diameter ranging from 13 to 17 micron. Our feral goats in Aotearoa New Zealand grow cashmere, and it was originally farmed for the fibre in the early 80s. The problem was they didn't grow much of it per goat, yet it's a highly heritable trait meaning production would increase rapidly with good breeding programs.

The Scots were famous for making the finest of cashmere garments, buying the raw fibre from Outer Mongolia. In 1982 they got very interested in buying cashmere from Aotearoa New Zealand to increase the supply and range of material with which they could work. They ventured Down Under and built up a relationship with the Aotearoa New Zealand producers, telling us that the price of cashmere never falls such as the luxury brand it was. The Lange Labour Government got into power in 1984, devalued the dollar, and goodness we were being paid up to $185/kg for this secondary follicle.

The world was our oyster.

That is, until the price of cashmere crashed around 1988. It would appear there was a price cycle for cashmere after all—it was just that it was a 30-year cycle, and people had forgotten that.

Now it was worth $50/kg—if you could find a buyer.

So a bunch of us cashmere enthusiasts thought to get together, buy up most of Aotearoa New Zealand's supply, make it into knitwear ourselves, and then sell it into the Japanese tourist market. 'Cloud 9 Cashmere' was launched with a capital injection by all the suppliers involved.

The numbers looked good. $50/kg makes three sweaters worth $200 each. A few costs of course, but on paper it was a no brainer.

We needed to find a designer—tick. A processor—tick. A knitter—tick. A market—tick.

Off we went selling garments under the brand name Sir Wam (very clever, apparently) in Rotorua, Christchurch and Queenstown to the inbound Japanese tourists. Guess what—it worked! It was very exciting to think we were actually making garments of enough quality that they would buy our expensive sweaters and scarves.

We held a fashion show in Auckland. It was very glamorous. I still have a full-length cashmere overcoat from that evening. Success can be intoxicating, especially when it comes out of the blue as it had.

There was one insight we had at this time though that was sobering. The rag trade is bloody tough. Every time you do something to the garment, the risks go up exponentially. For example, our cashmere got spun up into a yarn—you can use that yarn for only so many things. Then you dye that yarn, and now it's a particular colour and you need to have got that just right. Then you knit the garment to a particular style, and that needs to be just right. All of this is overseen by a fashion designer, who as it happens is not always great at detail and communication. Remember this bit—it turns up later.

Then the company directors thought we must grow this opportunity and raise more capital. Which they did with ease using a flash venture capitalist from Wellington, who not only raised more capital but also brought professional directors onto the board. We went from being a private company to an unlisted public company, which is a big shift in accountability.

We were off!

That was until the early 90's and the Japanese financial crash happened, and they didn't want to buy our pricey cashmere garments anymore.

Up until then I had just been a supplier of the cashmere and a shareholder of Cloud 9 Cashmere. Around the end of 1992, I was given the opportunity to join the board, which I was chuffed about. I was definitely the youngest and most inexperienced, so I saw it as an excellent learning opportunity.

We were farming up in Kaikohe in Northland at the time and had decided for multiple reasons to sell the farm and move south. We loved the area, but the marijuana trade in Kaikohe was huge and with the associated implications for the community we just didn't think it was in the best interests of the family to stay.

While we were living in Kaikohe I would drive down to Auckland for board meetings which I found fascinating—and this 33-year-old was definitely on a steep learning curve. It was apparent that our market was tanking and cash flow was drying up, and where we could do no wrong before, it seemed we could do no right now. However, I felt a sense of calm being surrounded by all this experience.

Until that is, the end of 1993 and the pressure was really rising. We had cut costs dramatically and used lots of other mechanisms to shore up the company. The professional calm of the experienced directors was showing some cracks. Then the venture capitalist with the endorsement of the rest of the board says she is willing to step in and complete a sales and marketing plan, get an arrangement with our creditors to kickstart the business again, and get us out of the slump. This was an expensive piece of work employing her skills, but it was going to illuminate a path forward.

The plan was completed. We had $600k of creditors in accommodation signed off (meaning they accepted the plan and would be patient while waiting for payment in time). We had $1.2m of stock on hand in our Christchurch warehouse or out in stores around the country.

We were alive and knew the way forward.

Who was going to execute the plan?

Well, I had sold our farm and had not bought another yet, had time on my hands, so the board suggested I step in as managing director to execute this plan. I was a bit tentative about the idea initially as I had really only experienced farming as a profession but was assured with a strong plan like this and support around me, I would be fine. We still had our fashion designer working full time, and she had plenty of experience. Everyone else involved in the leadership team was older than me by at least 10 to 15 years, and that gave me confidence.

The family were now living in Taupō, renting a place out towards Kinloch, which allowed me to start on my journey as a Managing Director of an unlisted public clothing company. Gulp.

The first thing I thought I needed to do is get out and about and catch up with the team in Christchurch. I arrived on a Monday morning to a very agitated designer who had weathered a lot of stress during the demise of the company. The last time I had seen her was at the fashion show in Auckland in totally different circumstances.

Of course, I went into complete information overload, and by Wednesday my head was spinning trying to make sense of what was going on. Then the farmer in me kicked in and I thought let's have a look at this $1.2m of stock on hand. I know about stock; it's what a farmer knows about. The designer was cagey when I asked to have a close look at the stock, saying "the venture capitalist has already done a stock take." I was so nearly thrown off track.

Nope, I wanted to go into the warehouse and have a reconciliation of what was on the electronic register and what it looked like in the flesh.

The look I got from the designer was of pure rage and indignation.

Item one: 25 Lilac crew neck cashmere sweaters knitted in type W style, $220/sweater.

"There they are."

"Cool," I said. "Let's count them together."

I was thinking to myself, *It's not fucken Sesame Street here, Harv.*

Nope, it was more serious than that.

We counted 22. Five were first grade, 10 were seconds, and seven were junk.

The monetary difference in value of those 25 sweaters—between what was in the grand plan I was to execute, and what we really had on hand—was $4,500.

There was an awkward moment between the designer and me when I asked, "Is this indicative of all the stock on hand?"

She was still defiant and said, "No, we have some wonderful valuable stock on hand."

"Then let's do a complete stock take right here, right now," I responded.

And that's what we did. And that's when I realised our quality control was shite because hidden in the inventory were seconds from four years prior that had not been written down in value. I learnt we could have sold even more garments when the market was humming, but we just had too many seconds.

I took a pen and paper, and for the next two days, recorded every sweater. I did the maths and learnt we didn't have anything like the $1.2m worth of stock, but instead $400k worth. I remember on a Friday afternoon in July in a warehouse in Christchurch, writing a handwritten report to the board and faxing it off to them, with my resignation at the bottom. I said I was sorry they had the wrong managing director because I couldn't possibly undertake this marketing plan. They needed someone of more skill than me.

You see, at that point I thought I was wrong. I was missing something. I was the inexperienced noddy amongst this group of experienced business people.

I flew back to Taupō feeling sick to my stomach and disappointed in myself, full of doubt.

The chair gave me a ring on Saturday morning and asked me a few questions to get clarity. He said they'd schedule a board meeting Tuesday morning on a conference call. The next few days my stomach churned. It's churning now just remembering that time.

10am Tuesday came around eventually, and I dialled in. I was sitting on the edge of our bed with my notes I had written next to me. There was the chair, the venture capitalist, and an independent director (he was working as a forensic accountant at the time on a thing called the Wine Box Inquiry), and me shaking in my boots.

The chair asks me to go through my two-page report line by line. I felt totally naked reading this out, with a tremor in my voice. Vulnerability wasn't a thing back in the 90's.

The chair thanked me and asked if there were any clarifying questions. There were a couple. He then asked the venture capitalist if she accepted my report. She said she did. That's when the independent director exploded and castigated the venture capitalist for lying to the board, and that he was sick of dealing with fucken professional liars like her in the Wine Box Inquiry.

The board went on to say they didn't accept my resignation and complimented me for doing a bloody good job in actually doing some groundwork.

Whatever I expected, it wasn't this. The meeting didn't last long after that, and the chair said we needed to reconvene ASAP and come up with a new plan.

My heart is pounding now remembering one of the most violent moments in my professional career. All of the faith I had in these experienced directors was shattered.

What followed was a 15-month lesson for me—and a deep one—as we wound down this company through an internal receivership and into liquidation. It was not what I had signed up for as an MD, but the lessons were perhaps even more valuable for my future.

Personal integrity and being authentic

I had no prior knowledge of the rag trade, but very quickly learnt some codes of practice and a lot about human nature. The only thing I realised I possessed of any professional value, was integrity and being authentic.

There was still a need to sell all the garments and extract as much value as possible for the creditors, wind down leases, and keep relationships intact to complete business.

When a clothing manufacturer is in the shite, they can use a system of having garments for sale in a store, where the store managers do not need to purchase the garments prior. Instead they sit on the shelves and the manufacturer only gets paid once the individual garments get sold in the store. The consignment model is one way of shifting stock because it frees up capital for the retailer.

We had our cashmere sweaters in a number of stores around the country using this system. Many of these stores were owned by Korean businessmen. Unlike the Japanese who were very fussy on detail and getting everything just right, then always paying on time, these Korean buyers were a whole different ball game. They were all about the short term, move fast, make cash, and didn't care about the relationship. They were mostly based in Auckland on Karangahape Road servicing the inbound Korean tourists who would be dropped to their stores in busloads. They would shop and get back on the bus and go to the next store.

That's how I got to meet Mr Steve Oh. Steve had about $80k of our stock through his store on the consignment arrangement. He still had some stock to sell in his stores. But I found that Steve hadn't been paying Cloud 9 Cashmere when he sold our garments.

So I made an appointment and went and visited him in his Karangahape Road office which was in a travel agency he also owned. His desk was right at the end in the middle looking down the corridor between the travel agent's desks.

His English wasn't brilliant (neither is mine) but after three hours we had an agreement of how much he owed us, which was $57k, with $10k still unsold. He said this wasn't a good time to pay, but he could pay $4,750 today, and the remainder next Thursday. I walked out with a cheque for $4,750 and thinking I had completed a good day's work.

I arrived in Steve's office at 8.30am on Friday of the following week and I wasn't in a very good mood. Steve saw me coming down the aisle and jumped up saying, "It's a bad time, bad time."

I replied, "It's a great time Steve. I have all day," and promptly sat down, put my feet up on his desk and said, "Get me a coffee please, I think I'm going to be here for a while."

He said, "I'm ringing the police."

To which I replied, "Let's ring them. Let's bring them in to hear this bullshit." (I regret to this day not doing just that—actually ringing the police)

Fuck, what a long day.

At 3pm I walked out with another $15k cheque.

We eventually took him to court for the rest and agreed to a progress payment plan of $10k every two weeks.

The first cheque arrived for $10k. I was hopeful. The second cheque arrived and it bounced. That's when I rang Steve Oh's office and got Interpol on the line instead.

So the next day, at 3pm, I met them in Steve's office. What a story unfolded. They had been after this bugger for years in many countries across the globe and hadn't caught him this time either. He had cleaned the Bank of New Zealand out of a few hundred grand, which made me feel better. Interpol told me I would not be receiving any more funds from Steve's business in the wind up.

They asked if we had any stock left in his stores. I said, "No we didn't." Which was technically true, because I had picked it up on the way to the 3pm meeting and had it in the boot of my car.

Learning from disasters

Those 15 months dealing with somebody else's mess was such a gift, even if it hadn't felt like that at the time. You learn way more when things go wrong than when everything is hunky dory.

I took the company through to liquidation without a single personal court case against me. It got close a few times, but I learnt deep down, don't bullshit; it will just bite you down the track. Don't over-promise, as people will remember what you don't deliver, more than what you did.

Having bad shit happen is not always a bad thing. Keep learning. That's always a possibility in any cluster fuck.

After 15 months on the road, I was keen to go back farming.

One of the most quirky things that happened to me through this foray into the rag trade is I got introduced to a Saville Road tailor who was based in Auckland. He was interested in some of our yarn we had in stock, and that's why we met initially.

I was fascinated to learn as much as possible about this mythical Saville Row, and so pestered him with questions. He was a Cockney and had all the mannerisms that came with that. I asked how he got on with the toffs, and he said he never really talked with them much, as he was there just for the fitting.

After a couple of meetings, he said, "Why don't I fit you out in some clothes?"

I scoffed; I didn't have the budget for it. His reply was fascinating. He told me the clothes are handmade, interchangeable, ageless, and because they last a lifetime, work out being very affordable. So I agreed and had a couple of jackets and pants made, along with a couple of silk ties. It was a big outlay up front, but he was right. I still have most of the clothes now, and they look new.

When it came to measuring me up, before he brought the tape measure out he summed up my body type and characteristics to his assistant as if I wasn't there.

But here's the thing. He said, "Broken right collarbone, needs padding to lift the shoulder."

Then: "Left knee has been operated on and will need pants to be altered to adjust to the walk."

I was amazed. I was still fully clothed. He went on to predict how my body would age according to my body type and having been a farmer. Most of this has turned out to be true.

Seriously. I was Harv in Wonderland.

I asked, "Where will the clothes be made?" Don't know why I asked, really, just interested.

His answer was another surprise. He said, "South of Te Kuiti, with a family down there."

"Why?" I asked?

"Well, Saville Row businesses have learnt not to have the actual tailors in London because they could be poached by competitors after giving them all training. Instead they train up families out in the villages where they were well paid and loyal and where competitors wouldn't find them."

I've learnt it's typical—you only get a glimpse of what is really going on from the outside looking in.

Reflections:

- Would others describe you as "being authentic"? Why?

- What have been some of the disasters or real disappointments you've experienced? What did you learn about yourself through these experiences?

Chapter 5

The Rob Moodie Effect—Values and critical rigour define effective decisions

"Of course policewomen should not get equal pay to policemen. How could that be feasible? They wear makeup and jewellery, get very emotional, aren't as reliable, and have periods every month. No it's not going to happen on my watch."

With that, the New Zealand Police Commissioner of the time got up and walked out of the negotiation room with his associates in tow.

At the other end of that negotiating table sat the newly elected Police Association Secretary, Dr Rob Moodie. He was expecting this and was not fazed at all. This was the late seventies, and you would be shocked at how backward we were in Aotearoa New Zealand in that era. It was a very male-dominated society.

At the next negotiation meeting, Dr Moodie came along wearing earrings and pale lipstick. Unfortunately, it was too subtle for the Commissioner to notice from the other end of the table. (Sounds like 'subtlety' probably wasn't his forte anyway.)

Not much progress was made at *this* meeting either.

So the third meeting, Rob came fully made up. His longish hair was in a woman's style, and he was wearing a bright dress. Rob also sported a moustache to round the image off.

The Commissioner apparently exploded and stormed out when he laid eyes on Moodie, to which Rob asked his stunned associates, "Is that a sign the Commissioner is agreeing to the pay rise?"

As it turned out, Rob wore the old boys down, and the policewomen received a 32 percent salary increase to gain pay equity for the first time in Aotearoa New Zealand's history.

This was the story I was listening to in a Sydney restaurant seated across the table from none other than Dr Rob Moodie, mid-1986. He was a wonderful storyteller, and I could listen to him for hours. His influence on me was profound, as I had never spent time with a celebrity like him before. His fame was generated by his complete disregard for convention, his love of women, and his disdain for the 'boy's ethos', as he called it.

Rob had been made a ward of the state at seven years old due to his father dying of tuberculosis and his mother struggling to feed the 10 kids they had. He was fostered by a farming family in Oamaru in the South Island. He struggled at school, didn't like reading, and left school at 15 to become a fencer and general hand.

At 19, he joined the Aotearoa New Zealand Police, and it was there that they found out his eyesight was not good—he got glasses and boom, he could read! Long story short, he then studied law at Victoria University graduating top of his class with first class honours, completed his PHD in 1976, then took on the Secretary role for the Police Association.

He held that position for 10 years and in that time became famous in Aotearoa New Zealand, often being in the news for his outspoken views on a range of issues. Notably, though, it was probably because of how he dressed that he got so much attention.

After the successful negotiation for the policewomen, he was told by the hierarchy to never wear a dress again, which got under Rob's skin. And then while visiting one of the Pacific Islands as part of his job, he realised the male police in Fiji were wearing sulus, which we might see as a dress of sorts. He then started researching other nations' dress codes and realised males wear kaftans and a whole range of skirts around the world.

So our Secretary for the Police in the late seventies started wearing Kaftans to public events, even drawing the ire of the Prime Minister Rob Muldoon, who called him "A queer crossdresser." People would ask him, openly, "Are you gay or queer?" to which Rob would answer, "Maybe—but how would you know?" Back then this was brave stuff.

Are we all 'goats'?

Why was I sitting with him in a Sydney restaurant? Well now that you've asked…

Somewhere in 1985 my first wife Annie was interested in goats and the cashmere fibre they produced. Meanwhile, Rob Moodie had got interested in Angora goats, farming them on his property in Long Gully near Wellington. We were introduced by a mutual friend of ours, and we got along splendidly (maybe because I was probably considered a bit strange too at that time).

This was during the heady days of the share market boom, and Rob was involved with a newly floated public company called Agricola. This company had a basket of companies involved in new farming trends like kiwifruit and Angora goats, and Rob thought they should also get into cashmere goats. So Annie and I started to look at how we might build up a superior cashmere flock. Annie had been on a guided tour of Australia the year prior where they were a few years more developed than we were in Aotearoa New Zealand with regards to cashmere.

Rob suggested that Annie and I share-farm with Agricola and build a flock together. Agricola would provide the capital, and we were to provide the expertise. Annie suggested we go shopping in Australia and try and buy some goats.

It was agreed. And we were given a budget of $250,000 to go buy goats. Annie was very good at building people's trust and we ended up in Northern New South Wales in a wee place called Inverell, being hosted by a lovely older couple who had developed a stunning flock of cashmere goats. They agreed to sell us some of their best goats, and we spent two days going through the small flock, selecting about 25 animals. All good.

We flew back to Sydney and were going to do some sightseeing. But instead we received a message from Rob at our hotel to give him a call. We found out that the farming couple in Inverell had changed their mind and now wanted to sell the entire flock for AUD$1m, or no deal.

Rob said, "Hop on the plane and be in Wellington tomorrow morning and meet with me and the Agricola CEO."

The next morning was a very intense situation for us two young country kids, being in this ivory tower with lots of suits, and Rob of course in his Kaftan. It soon became apparent that the share-farming deal was out the window, and that they wanted to buy the whole flock, and set up a farm in Australia. This was all decided in a matter of a couple of hours, and we were put back on a plane to Sydney that afternoon to now assess the entire flock and put the company ear tag on each animal.

These guys were operators! And we were now operators too!

That night in a Sydney hotel we were given a census form to fill out (because it was census day in Aussie) and one of the questions was, "How did you get to work this morning?"

I put down, "In a jumbo fucken jet." I thought my shit didn't stink at that moment.

We had gleaned from the meeting in Wellington that a farm would be purchased near Melbourne, and that raising the capital was not an issue. It turned out we had access to $65m if needed. WTF?

This proved to be the beginning of a fascinating look behind the scenes of a public company who were riding the wave of the 1986 stock market boom. At no stage were any budgets drawn up that made any sense of the investment, or how money was to be made from this helter-skelter strategy.

Agricola did buy a nice farm and sent an Aotearoa New Zealand fencer over to fence up the property. They also built a new Aotearoa New Zealand-style shearing shed. As the builders sat down in the homestead to celebrate its completion with a beer, a piece of metallic building paper floated on to the new electric fence. The Kiwi fencer had not turned the power down, which they do in Aussie to not cause sparks and a fire. The builders were alerted to the fire by the fire engine driving up the drive, looked out to see the wooden framed brand-new shed totally engulfed.

Oh, and it wasn't insured yet.

Well, of course, they just built another one.

Meanwhile the CEO was touring Europe (God knows why), spots a huge hay mower in Germany, and thinks we need one of those on the Australian farm. So he buys it. On arrival, it became apparent there is no tractor big enough within a few hundred miles to operate the thing.

You couldn't make this shit up.

The working arrangements at that time were that Annie was to be employed by Agricola, and I was to do some contract work. (It turned out I was to be the shearer of these goats in Australia—like they didn't have any shearers over there?)

By the autumn of 1987, the cashmere flock was in place in their new home. An intensive embryo transfer program was underway, whereby the top animals can be bred up quickly by harvesting embryos and planting them into other nannies (female goats). This is a very expensive process, and high risk.

So the shearer from Aotearoa New Zealand was called up, and I flew to Australia to shear a few hundred goats. Now I need to admit that I'm not even a good shearer—didn't like shearing goats, but what the hell, it was a giggle!

Of course, by the time I got to the farm, the locals thought we were a pack of incompetent noddies with too much money—a fair assessment, I'd say.

One of the most memorable events at this time was the flight home after shearing. I'd flown from Melbourne to Sydney and was boarding the flight to Wellington when I thought I noticed security fellas giving me the evil eye. I was in shorts, jandals (standard footwear in Aotearoa New Zealand during summer, and for tough Kiwis, winter as well!) and a t-shirt. I had literally no luggage; Annie was bringing that later.

I had no sooner taken my seat on the plane, when three police came up and asked, "Are you Ian Harvey?", which they'd got right.

Once that was established, they asked if I would accompany them off the plane. I thought, *What the hell is this shit?* so responded with a definite, "No." I could see myself missing the plane and all the inconvenience that would follow.

So they interrogated me while I sat there. As it happens, I've had this experience before—there apparently is another Ian Harvey about my age who had been a naughty boy for some time, and I've even had to respond to debt collector demands at times. It turned out he was now living in Australia.

The interrogation was not going well, until I had an idea.

"Look, chaps," I said. "I'm working for Rob Moodie—go give him a call—here's his number in Wellington." Rob, I knew, was well known in Aussie because of his work with the equal pay thing. So they did.

Ten minutes later they came back on the plane with my passport, apologised with a grunt (as only Sydney cops can), and let the plane go. The hostess came up to me with a glass of whiskey and said, "Looks like you need one of these." She was right. It was at that moment I thought drug smuggling is not for me.

All this time I'm thinking, *What we're doing with this goat stuff, it's all smoke and mirrors. How the fuck does this all work?*

Not long after this in June 1987 when the goats had finally got to Aotearoa New Zealand, Agricola had a stand at the Fieldays farm expo in Hamilton, displaying what we were up to and how to buy these wonderful goats from us. It was the longest three days of my life—manning a stand, answering questions from tyre kickers for something I didn't believe in anymore. Soul-destroying stuff.

Thankfully (for Annie and me), in October 1987, there was this thing called the Share Market Crash around the world, and Agricola (like so many other scam companies) was no more. The flash CEOs—ours included—were found out, and some even went to jail.

Put your ego away if you want to be truly authentic

What a wonderful education Annie and I had, without losing our shirts. It left an indelible stamp on me, because the behaviour of the leaders of the company was fuelled by ego—nothing more.

We remained in touch with Rob Moodie, and I feel very fortunate to have hung out with him for a few years. He instilled in me the idea that you can take on the system and win if you believe in your values enough.

He also showed me that if you don't have enough critical vigour surrounding you, it's easy enough to start believing your own bullshit and get lost in a make-believe world.

Annie and I came out with our reputations intact as we never strayed from the values we believed in, and Annie went on to develop a wonderful cashmere flock of her own of which we were very proud.

Reflections:

- Have you been involved in a project or scheme that may have seemed like 'money for jam' at the time?
- Did you perhaps feel some internal struggle between your values and the project's aims and method of operating? What alerted you to this? How did you handle it, and what did you learn?

Chapter 6

Collective Intelligence: Origins and Defining Moments — Don't pretend you've got your shit together — admit vulnerability

"What's it all about Harv?"

"What's what all about?"

"Life! I'm a 56-year-old professional woman and have everything I have been working for. And it sucks."

"Does it?'

"Yes—this corporate partnership is not bringing me any joy."

This was the conversation where I knew I was not only out of my depth, and at the same time I knew I was onto something with the model I had created.

It was the first turning point of my journey into the world of what was to be called Collective Intelligence. I was in my mid-thirties, pretending to be a facilitator with my first ever team.

Here's how I got there.

Back around 1993, due to my involvement primarily as an investor, I found myself a director of a number of companies. Of these, one was an unlisted public company (of which I was the MD) and another a private company. I was 33 years of age, eager to learn and very inexperienced. However, you have to start somewhere, and I loved the new challenge.

During this time as a director, I was fascinated that the biggest asset the companies had—and also the most limiting factor—were the CEOs. As a company director, you are there to represent the stakeholder's investment. And while this is essential, I thought that we were overlooking the development of the people at the top.

Sending them off to courses would often be stimulating, but resulted in little or no change as there was no follow up. These courses were an event, and not a process.

I read something once that sending people off to a training course was like polishing goldfish. They get all bright and shiny at the course, but then they're dropped back into the muddy waters of the organisation, and very soon they're all slimy and green again.

I thought, *maybe instead of trying to polish goldfish, there's an opportunity here.*

As a farmer back then I was very familiar with discussion groups where farmers exchanged technologies, ideas, and supported each other in their businesses. These farm discussion groups work because farmers are not competing with each other, and when they participate in well curated and facilitated groups, the value can be huge.

My initial idea was to put one of the CEOs into a non-competitive business group with other CEOs and founders from different industries. Generally when I have an idea, I think it's a good one. Back then I thought all my ideas were epic. I've lost that naivety with experience.

Off I went ringing mates I had been with at Lincoln, at school, and anyone whom I thought would be up for it. Bugger me, 90 percent said they'd give it a go. In no time I had eight people agreeing to turn up in Palmerston North for the inaugural meeting of what would later be called the Hornets. (No one liked the team name I gave—but didn't come up with an alternative, so Hornets it was.)

Now I just needed a facilitator. I had a great chap in mind by the name of Jonny Heslop (or 'Slops', as he was known then) and sat down with him to discuss the plan. I went through the concept with him, and he smiled and said, "Harv, they will all be a pain in the butt. In fact, you're a pain in the butt. You do it." What a motivational speech if ever there was one.

Now, the thing with Jon is he's an obstinate bastard, and I knew 'No' was a 'No'.

However, me facilitating the team was a stretch, pain in the butt or not. I said, "Jon, I've never facilitated before."

His reply was foundational. "Nope, you haven't, and nobody's been as stupid as you to try such a thing, so you are just the person for the job.

I will give you a couple of hours training and away you go."

That's what we did. I sat down with him and listened more intently than at any other time in my life. Here's the piece of advice that stuck to this day: "Start at the top of the mountain and work out how you got there. Then facilitate the team to the top of the mountain."

In theory, I almost believed I could do it. Until the night before they were to arrive in Palmerston North, and all my confidence vanished. Fuck that was a long night. The next morning the adrenaline started to kick in before dawn, and I thought, *Well, it's up to me.* Then I got to the building where the meeting was to be held, and I lost the confidence again—self-doubt in full flight. That was when I heard them starting to arrive, and I was dry retching in the toilet, thinking, *What the fuck did you want to do this for, Harv?*

Out of nowhere, an inner voice said, *Just be up front and say you are learning, and don't pretend to have your shit together.* What's the worst that can happen? That's what I did, and a piece of the culture was born, although the word vulnerability was not used back then.

The day sizzled with energy, and the shared issues they were all grappling with: imposter syndrome, cashflow, staff, lack of equity, anything and everything. I just held on and essentially was the timekeeper.

In the afternoon my first real facilitation issue arose. There was a bloke in the team called Smithy. He was an extreme extrovert and wouldn't stop talking—and we were running out of time. I tried several times to get him to stop talking, but to no avail. I was so frustrated, until I blurted out, "Smithy just shut up." And there was silence. *Oh dear, what have I done?* And then the room erupted in laughter; people were saying how it was brilliant, and carried on like nothing had happened. And another piece of culture was born. Authenticity—although that word wasn't used back then either.

This Hornet group stayed together for the next seven years and would test my skills and nerves like nothing I had done before in my professional life.

I copied the farm discussion group model, visiting each other's businesses—spread across the country—every four months or so. The members of the team were from different industries, but had a leaning towards the primary industries. There were seven white men, and one woman initially. It sort of represented diversity back then.

All through this time I was looking for a facilitator to take my place, but the team kept on accepting my presence, so I just stayed as the ever-lasting interim facilitator.

The learnings for me were constant, and a bit daunting if I reflected on them too long.

How the hell Harv, did you get away with being an amateur facilitator, without some sort of major calamity? The answer, I believe, is that the people I was working with were often pioneers themselves, and very forgiving. Even so, I still shake my head at the memories.

The whole process was evolving, and I sensed and responded by adapting different start and finish times, frequencies, intervals, focusses and the list goes on and on.

Then there were the curly seat-of-your-pants moments.

One was in Auckland, and the chap hosting had been showing us his empire of companies and assets he had bought with the proceeds. He was very ambitious and focussed on material gain. Through the course of the meeting, during dinner to be precise, the team had met his wife, and the women in the team (by now there were three women) took a special interest in her and her opinion.

We got to the end of the day and were ready for the feedback discussion, when one of the members asked if they could have some time alone without the host to deliberate. The host was more than happy and went off somewhere to amuse himself—counting his money perhaps?

Meanwhile the team were in a very reflective mood, pondering how to frame up the conversation that the host was not expecting. You see, he had indeed done a marvellous job of making money, and having the toys to prove it, but he was seriously deficient in his personal life.

Thirty minutes later, they invited the eager host back into the room and slowly, gently, described how they had viewed the world he created. They started with the positives. Yes, he was doing very well commercially.

Then one brave woman asked him to describe how he wanted to be remembered. The host pondered and then rolled out an eloquent response, which involved retirement with family and friends.

The gentle response was life changing. She replied to the host, "Well, you're not on that trajectory at the moment."

He was stunned.

"Look" she said, "you are a brilliant businessman, who is also very isolated, with no real friends, just acquaintances. You sponsor lots of things but connect with none of it. In fact, in this team, we feel you are here to impress us, not really connect with us."

And so the true and deep conversations began, which continued for the next few years as it turned out. Our host was shocked, but the feedback had hit a nerve, and the lights went on.

Some years later, his wife made contact with me and said, "Thank you Harv for saving our marriage." Now, I've had a few of those over the years, which are always deeply felt.

The other curly and defining meeting that comes to mind is the one described by the woman at the beginning of this chapter, "yes—this corporate partnership is not bringing me any joy."

The outcome of that conversation was me actually asking for help from a proper facilitator Jo Heslop (Jonny's wife—bastard still wouldn't help me!), who helped out with the framing of the day and co-facilitating the meeting. This meant we were able to explore the situation deeper than we previously had in the past. Jo then decided to hang around and joined as a team member of the Hornets.

After seven years, this team of pioneers was wound up with lifetime friendships established by some of the people involved. There were highs and lows within that period, and the range of topics and experiences were profound. From visiting a sheep and beef station on the tip of the east coast of the North Island, to learning about selling flowers in Auckland—the Hornets revelled in all of it.

Even though the team wound up in early 2002, the curiosity in me was set alight. And I wondered, *What would happen if we had multiple teams and stretched the diversity?*

And hence Collective Intelligence was born.

Reflections:

- Recall the time and place where you have felt most vulnerable—express the words (or better still, write them down) that describe how you felt. What did you learn about yourself from this experience? How has this impacted your personal and/or professional development?

- The word 'authenticity' has surfaced in this chapter and will do so many more times. What's your take on the need to be your authentic self?

Chapter 7

Collective Intelligence: The Early Stages—
The power of collective minds

"Harv, I don't know what goes on at your meetings, but my husband comes home a better man. Thank you. Have a well-deserved break."

This was the message on a Christmas card I received from the wife of one of our members in an early part of the development stages of Collective Intelligence. I lost that card in one of our office shifts unfortunately, but that message burns in my heart, and is very important to remember in some of the tougher moments of my journey.

Would I have begun Collective Intelligence if I knew the journey it has taken me on?

It depends at what moment you ask me that question, would be the answer. There have been weeks and months of despair and frustration. There have been months and years of pride, surprise and fulfilment.

What I do know is that I am a better person for it after 17 years of developing this concept.

What I also know is that it's been a far richer experience helping well over a thousand people on their own journey than I could have ever imagined.

You now know where its roots have come from with the initial Hornets team. Here's what happened next.

Around 2006, I'd had enough of farming and wanted to do something different. The something different wasn't (yet) Collective Intelligence. It was setting up a farmers' professional development standard. My reasoning was that professions like law or accounting meant you need to first become qualified, then you need to stay registered by maintaining a level of professional development.

Farming, on the other hand, is completely different. Anyone can manage vast areas of land, manage staff and produce food for the international market, with no qualification, and no regular professional standard needed at all. In my last years of farming I was overseeing around 3,500 ha of land with staff on three different sites in two provinces. I could see the complexity and scale building in farming businesses in the early 2000s and was not sure that the people on the land were keeping up with what was happening in the outside world—particularly in managing sometimes complex businesses.

I spent 18 months working on developing the concept of a 'Farmer Professional Development Standard' with lots of support from many quarters (none of which came up with any funding unfortunately). We visited the Minister of Agriculture, chairs of Dairy New Zealand and Sheep and Wool, plus some of the orcharding organisations. All the top-level people agreed there was an issue that needed addressing and saw the opportunity. If I was successful, Aotearoa New Zealand would have been the first country in the world to have a farmer management standard to guide their development.

But after 18 months of grinding away at the concept, I quit. The middle management of the farm bodies that service farmers weren't having a bar of it and blocked, blocked and blocked again. It was obviously going to threaten their status. So it was over.

Ironically, it's still needed, and still hasn't been done, and I see farmers still struggling to keep up with the rate of change. I believe other countries such as Ireland, have brought in such important systems.

Meanwhile, I had started the Bumble Bee Company with one of the original Hornets members, Nigel, to get the old model up and going as this learning process. This was the forerunner of Collective Intelligence. Nigel and I thought Bumble Bee was a grand metaphor for cross pollination. The name didn't last, thankfully.

By getting on the phone and ringing people, we got five teams up and going in 2008. An original Hornets member John gave me a list of 20 people to ring. Of that 20, about 15 people joined up. In those early days, we would take literally anyone, and the teams were still male-dominated, with a heavy provincial presence. Nigel was from a sales background, which meant we filled the teams quickly but with little finesse.

Nigel was going to be their facilitator—I mean, how hard can it be? Well, let's just say it didn't quite work out with Nigel as a facilitator in the first few months, and within 18 months our time working with Nigel came to an end.

This all worked out in the end. The Farmer Professional Development Standard hadn't fired up with the farmers, so I just pivoted over to the Bumble Bee Company. Rob was another silent partner, and he was interested in training the farmers and in what we were doing with Bumble Bee. As it happened, Rob opened the doors for some wonderful contacts in those early years. However, Rob pulled away after a time and focussed on his core business and I was by myself for a while.

Bumble Bee did have some early wins, which kept me fascinated with what was emerging. Our very first Host Day—where a CQ team member presents their business to their team to get feedback—was in Hawkes Bay with a farming company and its general manager as the focus. This farming company was a new initiative, stitching together privately-owned farms, and buying some other land to form a large farming entity all located in Hawkes Bay.

The general manager was a rock-solid operator, with his own family farm involved in the overall structure of other farms. The focus of the day was his performance as the GM. During the process, the team were introduced to the managing director of the company—a charismatic young man with a big vision—and another bloke who was an associate also with a big vision. They proceeded to tell our team what a wonderful smart business they were co-creating with wonderful projections and storytelling. All was going well until question time came around, and the power of an unbiased team of competent enquirers came into full force. In the end, I needed to stop the question time. It was getting embarrassing as the number of gaps in the answers were growing exponentially.

This was my first encounter of the destructive power of two creators (people who start organisations from scratch) coming together, riffing off each other, and building on each other's egos (and bullshit) with little to no challenge or critical thinking. This is a sure way of building the gross income fast with nothing actually dropping in the tin. It's something to watch out for, as it's not that uncommon.

These two chaps thought they were on fire the day the Collective Intelligence (CQ) team interviewed them. What this CQ team saw was smoke and mirrors, with all the alarm bells going off. It never ceases to amaze me what an unbiased competent team can see that others can't.

What transpired is that the CQ team quickly wrapped around the general manager and predicted the future of this company. The concept was excellent, but the execution was terrible. They suggested making sure his own personal assets were protected, and to start thinking about positioning himself as the future CEO. That second suggestion was a stretch at that particular point.

What played out over the next 18 months was a total collapse of this initiative, with something like $19 million dollars being written off leaving the company in tatters. This then paved the way for new investors to step in and, you guessed it, installed our member as the new CEO. Textbook outcome, with the newly appointed CEO staying on as a CQ member with us for another 10 years. I love these journeys!

However, this was a very lonely space for me during this time. Facilitation is hard. You can never get it quite right and you often hear about things that aren't good enough. Debriefing for the facilitator is great if you have someone to debrief to. I didn't.

But that was all about to change.

Reflections:

- What surprises have you had from perhaps unexpected feedback about your performance?

- How did this affect you? What did you learn?

- As a result, are there things you now do differently? What?

Chapter 8

Early CQ: The Powers of Listening and Emotional Intelligence—Being actively quiet provides true focus

3am is such an epic time for the subconscious to deliver information. I was so amped when it arrived. I had to text Jane then and there (you'll learn more about who Jane is shortly).

"I've got it!"

"What?"

"Why this team is out-performing!"

"I'm awake now!"

"They have three people in the team with a high emotional intelligence, and they lift the intensity of the conversation and hold it there longer than any other."

"Go back to sleep!"

Which I didn't, of course. I knew I was onto something and as it transpired, I still think I was right as we have studied other teams over many years to see what makes them tick.

You know by now that I went to Lincoln University for 12 months back in the day, and during that time met a wide range of people, being particularly drawn to a quirky crew who essentially liked creating fun out of nothing and at any time.

There was one young woman who really stuck out from the crowd of mostly young rural people. She dressed differently, had recently been involved in a commune and had a totally different worldview than most others. What was surprising for me was that this hippy chick and I got on. Her name then was Barbara Jane Adams.

Now Nigel (who'd later be a part of the Hornets) and Barbara Jane were an item at Lincoln and went on to get married and have a family. For a while, anyway, until they parted ways and Barbara Jane moved away from public life, setting up a retreat with an Indian guru in Nelson. (That's the place to do this stuff). I hadn't seen or heard from her for literally decades.

Until one day I get a text from her saying she's coming through Palmerston North and would love to catch up. I was stoked to hear from her, and catch up we did.

I found her in the town square sitting under a tree writing poetry. It would appear she hadn't changed much at all.

We quickly caught up on each other's lives, kids and stuff, and I learnt she was out of the retreat business now and looking to move back into the real world. She also told me her name was now Jane O'Shea, and the reasons for this change were complex—as was always the case with Jane.

I talked about my work at the Bumble Bee company. She was really interested and was keen to become a member to help her integrate back into the mainstream. The conversations continued over the next few weeks, and Jane mentioned that our website and messaging was shit. She could help with this: as well as writing poetry, she could write content as well.

What transpired was a partnership between us which brought a real richness and diversity to the establishment of Collective Intelligence. Plus a whole new intensity of learning, which apparently is called metacognition (thinking about thinking), since Jane brought a number of deep learning skills with her. She had also studied and was fascinated with the art of asking questions which is still very much part of the culture today, and I will be forever grateful for that gift.

Inspiring Questions

This opened up another tier of development we could integrate into our teams. Rather than giving advice, we developed each team's ability to use questions for other members to gain insight.

Giving advice is often not a very effective tool for helping someone in a difficult situation. The advice can go in skin deep, then ping off into the ether. However asking well-crafted open questions will take the recipient to wonderful spaces of insight, and insight is incredibly sticky. Once you have an insight, it just doesn't go away, and it's yours to keep even if it's hidden in your subconscious. This is the greatest gift Jane gave to me the time we worked together.

There were others as well. She introduced non-violent communication (NVC), in which she had done some training. NVC was developed by an interesting chap called Marshall Rosenburg, who grew up in Detroit during the 1967 riots and was inspired to study psychology. He then realised that wasn't fulfilling enough, so he went on to create a different way of communication based on universal feelings and needs.

NVC has four steps: Stating observations, then feelings, then needs, then requests. It's a simple framework that aims to find a way for everyone to share what really matters to them, and without any of those negative emotions like guilt, humiliation and shame.

The ability to listen

Now this was a monster stretch for me to learn. I had been brought up by a Christian mother where I learnt to fight to hold ground when we were in a conversation—not to be empathetic or give two fucks about how the other was feeling. I think I did about four of Jane's workshops before I started to get the hang of it. However, it is a hell of a way to hold crunchy conversations, and it taught me more than anything else—to listen. That's the lasting impact of NVC for me: the ability to listen.

If I asked you what makes a great communicator, you might think of wonderful orators, inspiring speakers, or a sage on a stage. Before Jane turned up, I would have answered something like that.

Now I would say a great communicator is someone who listens deeply and empathetically.

Many of the great leaders I believe didn't use more words than others. In fact I think they may have used less—that's my guess anyway. The great pieces of communication I have encountered in the past 17 years have been from people asking wickedly challenging questions, then being very quiet. I believe being actively quiet is a skill that few possess. I use 'actively quiet' because these people are listening intently focussing on what you or whoever is saying.

They are leaning into what is being said, and not waiting to start talking when you have finished speaking, they are just listening. Try it out. It takes practice.

I also believe the greatest gift you can give anyone at any time is to see them and hear them—actively.

Back to Jane.

Jane was the opposite of me in many ways. She was detail oriented and liked systems, writing policies and procedures and a manual. She understood my intuitive side. We were a very effective team.

Most of all, though, I now had someone I could riff off. This was the real gold, and something I crave to this day.

There was some weird stuff that came from Jane's past life from the guru retreat, like introducing me to the idea of coffee enemas. I'm not going into details here, but feel free to Google it in your spare time. Let's just say I didn't master this either.

I thought Jane might try her hand at facilitation, but it wasn't for her. That was a revelation because she had so many other soft skills. I had presumed she could take this on. As I have said before, it's not easy.

High Performing Teams

At this point I had created eight teams and was facilitating them all on my own. It's one way of becoming good at something—do lots of it.

One of the most impactful things Jane and I did together was start to analyse the performance of each of these eight teams. How were they tracking? What impact were they making? There was definitely a range in impact. One team for example was filled with high achieving individuals but were not helping each other nearly as much as other 'lesser' teams for example. We spent days pondering this off and on. The demographic of each team was studied looking for some hidden clue. Nothing stood out.

However, we had an outlier. A team that pushed each other more than any other, to achieve great positive effect. On paper they weren't special. What was it?

3am is such an epic time for the subconscious to deliver information. I was so amped when it arrived. As I wrote at the start of this chapter, and it's worth repeating—I had to text Jane then and there.

"I've got it!"

"What?"

"Why this team is out-performing!"

"I'm awake now!"

"They have three people in the team with a high emotional intelligence, and they lift the intensity of the conversation and hold it there longer than any other."

"Go back to sleep!"

Jane and I debated this for the next few months and when this team met again, I was conscious and observing if my hypothesis had any credibility. Sure enough one of the three would elevate a point via a challenge and the other two would help hold the pressure of the question or challenge. Gently, unconsciously, but consistently.

I only got this insight because I had eight teams on the go and could see the difference. Here's what I would see in comparison:

- Some teams didn't have the courage to mention the elephant in the room!
- If someone did, others would feel so uncomfortable they would break the tension with humour or a distraction.
- The high performing team would keep coming back to the issue and not move on until they thought they had enough information. Lesser teams would let it slide.
- The three High EQ members lifted the game of the other team members making them feel braver and supported to challenge a view.
- Finally, they put a higher expectation and scrutiny on my facilitation.

I was definitely watching an elite team in action, and it was very exciting to witness with some consciousness of what was in front of me.

The 'Emotional Intelligence' factor

A high level of emotional intelligence also has some of the following key signs and characteristics:

- Accurately guessing what other people are feeling.
- Noticing and describing your own emotions.
- Understanding your own strengths and weaknesses.
- Confidence in dealing with change.
- Being more likely to look for root causes of problems than to assign blame.
- Working well in a team.
- Coping well with pressure.
- Experiencing emotions without being overwhelmed by them.
- Predicting how other people will respond to a situation.

Did I say anything to the team? Nope, I didn't want to jinx them and break the spell. As it happened this team went on to outperform for years ahead, pushing each other to some wonderful outcomes. More on that later.

I tried to lift other teams to their level with a series of challenges and some clunky techniques like telling them they could push harder—but to no avail.

And diversity . . .

Then another observation started to drop into my consciousness. Teams with a higher ratio of women were also braver in the way they went about conversations. Now I am biassed in that I often prefer to work with women, but there was no doubt in my mind that the women in a team totally changed the conversations.

Here's an example I have witnessed often. Men were more likely to follow a dominant male's opinion, even if they weren't convinced of it, whereas women are less likely to be impressed with the male ego-led direction. I observed this numerous times with a woman quietly saying, "I'm not sure about this view." Sometimes this came late in the conversation as they had been pondering this view for a while. Then you would see others starting to support this woman's opinion seemingly changing their view from ten minutes prior.

A learning that has stayed with me for some time, is that I would not build any team without having a balanced female presence at the table if possible.

Collective Intelligence?

You may have been wondering by this stage, just where did the name Collective Intelligence come from?

I was facilitating a team in Wellington and one of the chaps in the team had just come back from an extensive training program in France with a flash outfit called INSEAD, the business school of the world. That's a statement! It was a big investment to go to INSEAD, and I was very keen to learn as much as he would share.

During this program they measured a number of things:

- His IQ (Intelligence Quotient)—which was above average
- His EQ (Emotional Intelligence Quotient)—which was below average
- His PQ (Physical Intelligence Quotient)—which was slightly below average

He said that because his EQ was low it was affecting his ability to mobilise the team and delegate effectively. Because of that his PQ was being affected because he was working longer hours.

He also shared many other aspects from the course which were all very interesting, but I wasn't really listening because I had locked onto what would it mean to have these Q's interlocked somehow, and bingo I came up with CQ—Collective Intelligence. Now over time it has become more in depth than this, but that was the genesis.

Reflections:

- Chances are that you've been a member of a high-performing team at some stage. Think back (or if it's one you're currently in) what is it that made that team so successful?

Chapter 9

Fuck, Harv, has no one got their shit together? —
Is the pain of failure too high to face up to reality?

It was mid-February, and we were in downtown Auckland at the BNZ Centre at the start of a day and a half full of a Collective Intelligence Host Day. I was one of the two facilitators. I could sense the team was excited to come and get under the bonnet of what we believed was a state-of-the-art business from one of their team members. (Host Days are where the CQ team looks extensively at one team member's organisation and provides the Host with feedback)

The host in question had a TV show dedicated to his passion and was on lots of other media channels as well. The host knew his stuff and spent a lot of time telling people how to do 'the thing' to make lots of money.

To say we were in awe of this person's accomplishments would not be far from the truth. I put in extra time preparing for the meeting to make sure we did the topic justice.

The question that the host put to me was this: "I've got a very good handle on the business and where it's going—keen to learn if I have any areas I can tweak."

I thought, *Let's go all in* and asked if it would be okay if I organised mystery shoppers who were in the market for these high value products. "Absolutely," he responded confidently.

The stage was set. We were primed to learn how a super smart high-end business operated.

It started slowly as we gleaned information from interviewing various people associated with the business. The team I could see were struggling to recalibrate as the information came in, and I kept reminding them to trust the process, stay open, be curious and gather information with great questions.

They did. Then the mystery shoppers entered the loop. One of the shoppers was actually in the market for these products at the time and had put way more effort in than, I thought. I trusted this person's judgement highly.

After four hours of discovery, the team was left with a train wreck. Nothing was as it was portrayed. We were all a bit shaken by the experience, because the hard part was yet to come—the feedback to the host. He had not been present during the interviews (a system we use to glean unbiased information), so with what we'd learned, the feedback session was going to be a tough gig.

But before we prepared to deliver the feedback one CQ team member jumped up and said, "Fuck Harv, has no one got their shit together?" I have never seen a team member so perplexed. He was clearly agitated.

I replied, "It would appear not."

The feedback was gentle, generous and fraught. The so-called tweaks were in fact great big black holes. The host was in disbelief and tried to undermine the team and facilitator's credibility, saying we just weren't sophisticated enough to gauge the situation accurately. Then he walked out the door never to rejoin the team.

I spent weeks in conversation with the host after this to make sure he was okay, and to see how I could assist—to little effect, other than to take some well-honed criticism at me.

I've seen similar situations (perhaps not quite so dramatic) play out numerous times over our Collective Intelligence journey to one degree or another.

Reflections:

- What do you think about when having to give some feedback that you know will be hard to take or indeed accept?

- How did this affect you? What did you learn?

- As a result, are there things you now do differently? What?

Chapter 10

Our Backward Bureaucracy—Is efficiency different to innovation? Is one way more valuable than the other?

Slap. That was the noise of a 700-page document hitting the desk in front of the Minister of Justice and Cabinet Minister for the National Government at the time.

"Adopt this into law, Minister, and you will make a positive impact of between $2.5 to $4 Billion dollars per year to the New Zealand economy."

Silence… I mean, what do you say to that?

I thought this was going to be an epic news story. However, what unfolded over the next six months is a story that I wish was unique in Aotearoa New Zealand. As it turns out, it's not.

A year earlier on New Year's Eve, on a beach in Hawkes Bay, I was introduced to an extraordinary woman by the name of Prue. Prue was English and had moved to Aotearoa New Zealand because her Kiwi husband had got a job in Wellington. At the time of meeting Prue I thought she was pretty smart. I was right and wrong at the same time.

Prue was intrigued by my work at Collective Intelligence and was keen to join one of our teams, which she did early the following year.

She started tentatively with her Collective Intelligence team, which was already established, feeling her way into their culture. Prue, we learned, was schooled up in the world of intellectual property (IP) and had been involved in lots of projects internationally. There were some very smart cookies in this team, and even they were struggling to understand all that Prue talked about in the world of IP.

Prue's world view was vastly different. Her language was different, and she challenged the norms. Prue was quite forthright to some of the privileged men in the team, pointing out that, "being the cream of the crop of a very dull industry didn't mean you were all that smart." She would often point out efficiency was different to innovation, and one was way more valuable than the other.

Prue often lamented that Māori were way more up with the play of IP due to the fact they shared IP and kept the wheels of innovation turning, whereas Pākehā tended to try and protect it and stall innovation.

Over the next twelve months, the intrigue by her CQ team members grew about Prue's work and the world she inhabited. Their understanding didn't, however. There were question marks appearing around her competence as a result of the team not 'getting' her.

That all changed when she hosted her team in Wellington, and as usual I had arranged a group of her peers that could shed light on her abilities, connections and competencies. On the initial list of interviewees was a name I can't remember, but a title I could: CEO of Disney. Like, *CEO of fucken Disneyland* was on her list to interview? But for some strange reason he unfortunately wasn't available, his EA told me. I hadn't shared this with the team prior to the meeting, as the interview hadn't happened, so left it out.

However, we did interview a businessman from Aotearoa New Zealand who almost scolded the team for their low bar questions and in the same breath let us know that Prue was regarded as one of the top 50 international IP specialists in the world. He then asked if the CEO of Disney was being interviewed, as he and Prue were best of mates. I said no, because he was busy, to which the businessman simply said, "Busy!"

After that particular interview, we stopped for a cuppa, and one of the members said, "We were wrong—so wrong about Prue," to which there was a murmuring of agreement.

We also learned that Prue had been part of the team who had developed the IP standards and laws for the G7. That apparently was a big deal.

Here's the learning for me…

When someone is way smarter than you or the pack, they can seem dumb. Keep that in mind next time you don't understand someone. *You* just might not have the smarts, not them.

So after Prue's Host Day, the team had a whole new appreciation and perspective. They got that she was world class—finally.

Prue had also informed us that she didn't register any IP in Aotearoa New Zealand, such was the laxness of our laws at the time. I was a bit shocked to hear this, and on further enquiry, found that she could help rectify that if she had access to the right people. I soon learnt who those right people were and organised a hui (meeting) for her.

It was set up in Palmerston North with the then Minister of Justice (who was our local MP) and the Minister of Trade.

In the interim we had worked with Prue developing her communication skills to be able to talk to these blokes in a way they could understand—in essence, dumb it down a notch.

The scene was set in a suitable meeting room, with the two Cabinet Ministers and a hanger-on politician included (not sure why). I got everyone to introduce themselves and then a brief of why we were here. Prue then launched into the opportunity that she saw for Aotearoa New Zealand to come up to speed with the G7 nations' IP laws by adopting their standards, and what impact it would have on our economy.

She nailed the presentation in six minutes. It was a masterclass in delivering clear information in a concise way. I felt so proud to be in her presence at that moment.

Then the Minister of Trade asked Prue what her academic qualification was. She said she had a PHD in international IP law, but stressed she wasn't a lawyer.

"Where did you gain this PHD," he asked.

"Cambridge University," she replied. "But I'm not an academic—I work commercially adding value to companies and being paid for the value I provide. I don't sell my time."

Then there was this odd uncomfortable silence as it appeared the politicians had run out of questions to ask or things to say. It was a bit embarrassing, I have to say.

That's when Prue stood up, picked up a large book and walked around to where the Minister of Justice sat, who hadn't asked one cohesive question, and said to him, "Adopt this into law Minister, and you will make a positive impact of between $2.5 to $4 billion dollars per year to the Aotearoa New Zealand economy."

Talk about making an impact—I would pay money to just watch this unfold again. It was brilliant!

So the Minister mumbles and jumbles and agrees to get the wheels turning in Wellington with the appropriate bureaucrats. I was feeling very happy with the result, and thought this was a coupe.

Well it was another lesson in naivety on my part, and Prue's to a lesser degree.

Prue was introduced to the correct bureaucrats by the Minister of Justice, and we assumed the wheels would begin turning to adopt the most modern IP laws in the world for little Aotearoa New Zealand.

But instead what happened was a retaliation and rejection of Prue by the Wellington system, inferring that she was yet another consultant who was just interested in clipping the ticket. Prue stressed she was doing this for free, as a gift to her adopted country.

I would receive phone calls from Prue in tears of frustration, and anger from being bullied and put down by these bureaucrats. I followed up with the Minister, but was confronted with a new piece of information, in that there was actually fuck all he could do to influence these people. I was gobsmacked and have since learnt this was not an isolated case and still goes on to this day.

The upshot is that Prue lost a huge amount of confidence in her own value and what she was offering. What I am so proud of is the support she now got from her Collective Intelligence team in building and supporting this genius woman, which became important as Prue was asked to present at the next Asian Pacific Economic Cooperation summit (APEC)—on the topic of international IP law, of course.

Here's the irony. She delivered another masterclass presentation to the Chinese officials present. They asked her to join their team, and said she could live wherever she wished, and they would honour her work and guidance.

Prue now lives in Paris, working for China, last time I heard.

Meanwhile I followed up with our local politician and Minister of Justice to give him the news. It went okay until he said, "Win some, lose some." I won't repeat what my response to him was.

One of my biggest frustrations in Aotearoa New Zealand is this gap between bureaucracy/bureaucrats in Wellington and business people. It has to improve. It is a major impediment to our country's future, and I have no idea how to improve the issue. I have voiced this frustration to many people in the know and there is a general acceptance that the system is broken.

I have floated the idea that one of our Impact Teams could help change this. Is anyone listening? (Impact Teams are a reasonably new initiative at Collective Intelligence, where we set up teams within one organisation based on cross-functional experience/expertise and diversity).

Reflections:

- Can you recall an instance where you met someone who on first impressions was not too smart, only to be proven wrong later by their 'smarts'?

- How has this experience affected the way you now view new team members, colleagues and even potential partners?

Chapter 11

Diversity Started to Raise its Head —
The power of different thinking

"Harv, I would like to become a facilitator with Collective Intelligence."

"Not looking like that you're not."

This was my response to Manda Johnson who had just attended a facilitator training with me that Jane had organised in Wellington. I remember the date was 23rd February 2011, the day after the Christchurch earthquakes.

Manda had been living in a community in Golden Bay at this stage in her life and had hair down to her waist, wearing what I would call hippie clothes. I thought Manda would never facilitate for us in a million years. But my goodness she seemed determined and said, "Whatever it takes I want to work with you." I was a bit flattered and amused all at the same time.

So I said, "Well okay, let's give it a go—but first of all, you need to look a bit more mainstream."

A month later Manda met me in Hunterville in the Rangitikei Region. Her hair was shorter and she was wearing different attire, and she was to hang out with me while I facilitated a CQ team hosted by a farmer. I thought this would be a tough test for this hippie. Manda took to it like a duck to water. The team were intrigued with her back story and where she lived, but otherwise received her as the professional she was. Plus—and this was a big plus, she would offer the odd pointer to me of how I might lift my game as I facilitated.

We were then three years into the business when Jane introduced me to some of her other colleagues from the Wellington region where she lived, some of whom became facilitators in these early years. Notably

Pamela Meekings-Stewart, Sue Johnstone and of course Manda Johnson. This was epic, because I had never had facilitator buddies before and these women possessed skills I didn't even know existed.

Think about it. I had facilitated the first team for seven years by myself, and the first three years of the Bumble Bee company also solo. All I had to do now was get them initiated and hand some teams over to Pamela, Sue and Manda.

While this was going on, something else was too.

We had grown through word of mouth and our focus was on the business sector—diverse businesses all around Aotearoa New Zealand, but all commerce based.

Then a farmer suggested I contact someone from the education sector and I was lukewarm. So I ignored it. It's a good strategy. Try it! Then this chap's name came up again as a referral, and I thought, *Okay let's give it a go.*

Next thing I'm sitting in the principal's office at Palmerston North Boys' High School thinking how I've never enjoyed being in this space. But mostly I'm in doubt as to whether a school principal would fit in one of our teams. The school wasn't a business. It wasn't a fit.

That's how I'm feeling as I talk with Tim O'Connor, the well-known rector of the college. The conversation was a bit stilted until I spotted a book on his bookshelf—*Good to Great* by Jim Collins. It was a book we'd used often in the early days to help guide us and introduce us to our members. It's a great book about great commercial organisations. I asked Tim if he had ever actually read it.

He jumped up and pulled it off the shelf stating, "This is my bible." And sure enough it had bookmarks all through it.

I thought, *You beauty, let's go!* and Tim joined a new team that was forming a few weeks later.

Their first Host Day was in Hawkes Bay a few months after starting. It focussed on a boutique food business, co-owned by a young man on a mission, who was our member. Pamela Meekings-Stewart was with me as part of her facilitator initiation. It was an exciting time, all these new beginnings.

The host had given us his focus of: How could he grow sales by

20 percent in the next two years?

Now we have learnt at CQ that the issue is never the issue. This was to be no exception.

The team toured the modern plant and got a good feel for the product. They were warming to the task at hand and all was on track. Until that is, we interviewed this young man's majority shareholder and business partner, who was very prickly being asked questions from the team. She stated at one point that her husband was a lawyer and that she didn't have to answer the question. Tim the school principal replied, "Well, you just have."

It went downhill from there, and the interview ended soon after. I was a bit shaken, but then Pamela stepped up and said, "It's all information. Nothing more, nothing less. We are here to collect information." She was spot on.

The feedback to the host was the shortest in our history.

One line. Six words.

"Sell your shares or buy hers."

He was completely silent for what seemed an eternity.

"Why?"

This is where Tim was brilliant. He said, "I have 127 staff, and don't have anyone as destructive as your business partner. If I did, I would have them removed at any cost. You have her as a majority shareholder and you are in for a life of bullying and misery. You are 33 years old with your life ahead of you. Either you go, or she does."

That's a hell of a message to receive.

Oh—the irony was that his business partner was the instigator of him joining Collective Intelligence!

What came from that?

Our host accepted the advice and received a huge amount of support from the team, buying his business partner out. He then hired her back as a contractor and they got on like a house on fire.

Meanwhile, another couple of switches went off in my head. If a school principal could add so much value into a team, who else could? The other was that I was starting to understand the power of unbiased feedback. It's rarer than you realise. More on this later.

Our first big gig in Auckland happened around this time.

We had a chap join from a flash company where he was the CEO, and he put his hand up to host the team. His focus was on how to raise the functionality of his organisation—a professional service provider. The CEO had come from the corporate world and was frustrated by the lack of collective performance from this company of individual high performers.

I was facilitating, with Manda on her second trip away with me to learn the ropes. Both of us were on edge going into this feeling a little out of our depth. To make things worse, my plane from Palmerston North—on the Thursday—was delayed due to fog in Auckland, meaning me and others needed to fly to Hamilton and get a bus for the final stretch arriving mid-afternoon. Luckily the Host Day itself was on the Friday, and we could start the next morning on time.

Friday morning arrives after a bad sleep for me, and we walk into this mahogany-covered office with photos of past boards and other memorabilia, staff in their suits and ties. It didn't help my nerves, I can tell you.

Now a bit of background re the dress code. I have always encouraged that people wear whatever makes them comfortable. So our CQ team as per normal is walking into this shrine of elegance casually dressed to start our day of interviews.

We had a tight schedule in front of us and were ready, having had a good briefing the night before. The CEO had stated one of his frustrations was that he didn't think business partners actually understood the company structure, chain of command, or even respected him as CEO: he wasn't of their professional background. So the CQ team's job was to understand from a selected group of six partners their views on these key areas. The selection had been made by the Chairman of the board—otherwise I'm not sure they would have fronted.

The day got underway with the first interviews. What struck us initially was the beautiful suits these chaps (there were no female partners) turned up in. They were very well groomed and had an air of talking to peasants because they had to.

We had worked out a system where the first five questions were standard and asked by the same people in a particular order, then we would go off script from there.

Number four question was being asked by a very experienced woman by the name of Ally, who had lots of bouncy flaming red hair. Her question was, "Who are you accountable to?" A reasonable standard question in an organisation like this.

By the time we had interviewed the third partner, Ally had got three different answers. The others had too on the fixed questions, much to the surprise and mirth of the CQ team. It was apparent the partners were very skilled at responding on their feet.

The fourth partner gave us yet another: "I'm one of the respected practitioners in my field in the country, I'm accountable to myself." Ally chuckled at this, then smiled demurely and wrote down the answer. Meanwhile I'm sitting at the front of the team scowling at her as she was starting to glow with humour.

Partner number five comes in and Ally has got the giggles even before she gets to her question. It's quite apparent none of the partners had any idea how the company actually worked. She is bright red and glowing sitting in amongst the rest of the team who are trying to ignore her infectious giggling. She couldn't do it, couldn't get the question out and excused herself and went off to the ladies' room to calm down. Fuck it's funny looking back now, but I was mortified in the moment thinking we would get told off.

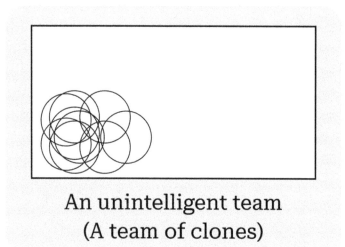

An unintelligent team
(A team of clones)

Ally came back as partner number six arrived for his interview. I remember distinctly that he was wearing a very bright yellow tie and was more relaxed than the first five. He was hilarious as he play-acted that he knew the answers and treated it like it was a big game, then came clean that he had no idea and that he wasn't really that interested. "I'm a good practitioner, do my thing, get paid well and go home," he said. He was the first bugger that wasn't bullshitting us.

He then asked if we wanted a tour of the facility, which we agreed to as we were done with the questioning. The other thing that stood out was that he appreciated the time we were taking to help the business. It was a positive way to wrap up the session, and we all reflected that none of us could have predicted how that process was going to pan out.

The team had a break and then came back for deliberation and feedback to the CEO. It was surprisingly easy as it turned out, given the commercial experience in the team, and once again a team of unbiased people could see the situation clearly. It was not complex.

We fed back the finding to the CEO who was very appreciative, as it confirmed and highlighted his views (this is not always the case believe me).

The next step was a stretch in my confidence as I then needed to give this feedback to the Board Chair, which I did initially in writing, and then a follow up meeting with him. I was apprehensive leading into the meeting. This was my personal insecurity playing out.

As it turned out I shouldn't have been.

He started off thanking me and the team, and then asked how a group of civilians could come into a business for a day and deliver such succinct and accurate feedback. It was the first time I used this phrase, "It's the power of Collective Intelligence." What's more, I truly believed it.

Reflections:

- What approach do you take when you think someone is bullshitting you?

Chapter 12

Building Your Personal Base — And having external, invigorating interests is also important to your well-being

"There's no bloody way that's happening. If you are okay with our help, we can get this sorted by Tuesday morning."

We were sitting in a café in Nelson for breakfast on a Friday morning, with the CQ team Skyping into a CG team member in Wellington who could not make the team meeting. Why? Because she was so distraught and stressed, she didn't have it in her to attend the meeting. She was about to lose the controls of the company she had painstakingly brought to life mostly by herself.

Her co-founder, who had lost interest in the company due to the struggle of it all, was back from travelling the world and now living in Australia. As we were hearing via Skype, he was bullying our CQ scholarship member, angling to buy her out for a pittance due to some legal loophole. The details are not important. He was about to succeed. Or so he thought.

The CQ team were a mix of highly experienced business owners and a lawyer, and they were furious. They had seen how hard she had worked for little to no financial gain and yet had created so much benefit for others.

She accepted our call tentatively at first, but then was on board by the end of the discussion. Simply put, the team said they would draft all the emails to this chap and send them to her for approval. She'd then email these messages to her co-founder.

It must have been a shock for the co-founder to start suddenly receiving vastly different toned emails. By Tuesday morning he had signed an agreement and for a small investment our scholarship recipient now had full control and 100 percent shareholding in the business—which is still doing wonderful work to this day.

Building your Personal Base

Why do I mention this story?

It's a great example of what can happen when your personal base is not built robustly enough to cope with your success and challenges. And this is where our CQ team had become her personal base.

Through this time, I was learning more and more about startups, and just how tough they are on the founders. Generally they are best suited to people from privileged backgrounds, because the chance of getting things right the first time are fuck all. That's where 'pivot' comes in, right? And each time you pivot you can lose equity, and or a percentage of shareholding.

All the time you're pivoting, your personal base is being challenged. Why am I doing this? Why did I leave my salary? My status has evaporated. My friends don't know what the fuck I do anymore, and I'm always tired, and so on.

Or you are getting epic social media coverage, on the telly, in magazines, winning competitions for your new idea and rocking the world. While behind the scenes you are anxious, not sleeping because of poor cashflow, and you are not loving the total absorption the business requires.

I smile to myself when people talk about, the wellbeing of founders and how we need to get better at work-life balance, and how supporting these wonderful people is simple.

Fuck it—I'm going off track here, but hey it's a Saturday morning as I write this, and I've got a gastro bug and I'm grumpy.

Being a founder is a type of disease that so far is undiagnosed, in that it doesn't have a medical definition—yet. A bit like how ADHD 'never existed' until a few years ago. We have worked with scores of founders in many industries. They are amazing people and seriously fucked, all at the same time. They literally believe their creation will do something special that no one else has done before. And some succeed. But when we talk about supporting their wellbeing like they are normal human beings, we fall into the trap of coming up with a simple solution to a complex beast.

I've been on the phone numerous times to founders who are wanting to end their lives due to burnout, stress and disillusionment. They will push themselves to the point of utter exhaustion—repeatedly, just to bring their idea to fruition. I know. I'm one of them, and I've felt like that too.

It's not normal nor admirable at times. But there are periods where we just can't help ourselves, such is the conviction of the movement that has been unleashed. I've not seen this expressed consistently in any other group other than founders. One day Collective Intelligence will learn more about this phenomenon, but for now we are grappling to keep up and nurture them as best we can.

Social media doesn't help either. Numerous times I've seen members on the socials smiling away and posting about the amazing day they have had achieving some milestone, while I know behind the scenes it's nothing but rubble. It doesn't help those also in the rubble pile, who look on at the founders and only see a smiley face. Founders are getting way better at sharing what's really going on, when they are feeling resourced enough. And that's the important bit: resourced enough.

From experience, founders tend to spend 80 percent of their time with their backs against the wall in the first five years, maybe longer. That's what it's really like. For example, I took a call from a founder of a wildly successful organisation one day which had been going for a dozen or so years. She was distressed because a corporation had targeted her general manager with an employment package that they could not meet. She said, "I wouldn't have started this venture if I knew I would still be needing to fight these battles after all this time."

As it turned out, the GM didn't take the role, which was a show of dedication to the company. However, that pain was real at the time.

Where was I?

Oh yeah, building your personal base.

We are taught technical stuff in our education system—knowledge about 'things'. Things that mean sweet fanny in the world of being a professional, or founder. It's changing slowly, I know.

However, you need to learn and build on your EQ if you want to be a founder. Perhaps learn a musical instrument and learn a form of art. This will help build the breadth of base needed to keep your wellbeing more in order. Breath work, yoga, and meditation also need to be incorporated into your personal development if you want a life outside developing your grand idea.

Plus, we need to have a little more compassion for founders in Aotearoa New Zealand. I have literally heard an angel investor at a conference say, "Not another fucken founder." This investor had made his money in the corporate world and invested in property, which is a million miles away from startups. I moved on as I could not be bothered with his ignorant attitude.

One more thing that irks me in the startup world. We dilute the founder's shareholding way too much during a capital raising process, particularly in high tech companies. Nurture and love those crazy founder people and you will get way more from your angel investment in the long term.

As I write, I've still got the gastro bug but feeling much better getting that off my chest.

Back to the personal base.

The amount of pain you are willing to endure for whatever you want to take on will be directly proportional to what you are able to create.

I have an old mate whom I refer to as an 'inventor' more than an 'entrepreneur'. I might be wrong about the distinction, but it's my view.

His name is Andy Ramsden. I have known Andy since my time in Rathkeale, although we weren't close then. I got to know him more by chance when we ended up shepherding on the same property in Taihape. I was finishing my 18 months when Andy arrived to take my place. We were—and still are—chalk and cheese in so many ways. Very alike in others.

While shepherding, the boss's wife took an intense dislike to me, which on reflection, I think was justified. Andy turned up and she thought he was lovely. Boys will be boys and, Andy and I had a wager as

I was leaving for Lincoln. "I reckon I can get into the boss's wife's pants by the time I'm finished here," said Andy.

"You're on!" I replied. "$50 you can't."

In September that year I got a letter in the post saying, *She's pregnant, send the money.* (Before lawyers are called—it wasn't his!)

Anyway Andy was just a fun-loving guy with a wicked sense of humour and a love for practical jokes which I have often been the butt of. Bastard. He was destined to become a farmer in his very able father's footsteps.

But something changed in him in his late twenties. He came to be obsessed with sheep genetics. I mean, like *obsessed.* To the point of being a complete pain in the arse at times. Forty years on, it hasn't left him, and he has been on a rollercoaster of a ride to say the least.

He has invented new breeds of sheep for many different functions and been at the cutting edge of genetic technology all that time. It has cost him his health, his relationships, and he's often been ostracised by the very conservative rural industry at times. The irony is that if he had been working in the IT world, they would have appreciated him. Farmers have not.

Anyway, the point is this. Andy's ability to withstand the immense pain of financial insecurity at times, and of doubters of these ideas shunning his innovations, has meant that after forty years he is starting to kick some serious goals in a number of areas. He has finally got people around him of a calibre that can harness his genius visions, which I am so pleased to see.

He now has a good personal base.

He's 66 years old at the time of publishing this book, and still out there working on a new idea, with previous ones now bearing fruit. I doubt he will ever stop. My wish is that the sheep farmers are able to comprehend just what he has achieved for the industry.

He is not uncommon in the founder space.

I took a call from a CQ member (a founder) one afternoon. She was in tears of frustration due to a capital raise coming down to the wire, plus a number of other shit storms.

"It's such a struggle," she said.

My reply wasn't what she was expecting, but I thought it was useful.

"Humans are designed to struggle, so dust yourself off, chin up and get the capital raise done—and worry about the other stuff later."

I think I might have got a "Fuck off" in response to that, but she did as I suggested and thanked me later.

We have had a few rugby All Blacks through our program, and I asked them what's the difference between the different levels of rugby competitions. One said, "There's more tears the higher the level." I wasn't expecting that.

The message behind all this? If you are going to take on anything big, the first thing to do is to build a big personal base to work from. Then you need to have a reasonably high EQ. Now, this doesn't mean you're not going to get upset or feel down at times. Instead a solid personal base and a good EQ allow you to recover quicker. It's a bit like getting physically fit. You still get puffed, but your recovery is more rapid.

Build your personal base and go do the training that will expand your EQ. Practice having brave conversations. Learn how to give and receive feedback. Learn to listen actively. This list could be endless but if you don't get the picture by now you may well not get it anyway.

Learning a discipline

The other base that I believe is easily overlooked is that of a good old-fashioned grounding in a profession, regardless of what it is. Learning the discipline of a trade for example, teaches you process and context. It was something I lacked in my early years of farming as I went to the home farm after one year of Lincoln because of my father's poor health. I would have benefited by having a few more years growing up and learning from others instead of going home at 20 years old. Luckily, I'm a curious bugger and got off my chuff and learnt as much as possible from excellent farmers.

Side subject: I also think learning another trade outside of what you were intending to focus your life's work doing would help greatly too. For example, I believe farmers would benefit from being involved in the service industry to learn what it's like to serve customers one-on-one.

This issue of not having a professional base raised its head out of the blue for Jane. She was holding a seminar on NVC one day in Palmerston North. Attending the course were some people from scientific backgrounds. They started probing her about where this had come from and where she had studied this.

The truth was that Jane was self-taught and doing a pretty good job of delivery. But, and it's a big but, hadn't trained through the NVC system.

The science-based people kept probing and, in the end, continued with the day, but Jane's bubble had been burst. The were not happy to be sold a professional development session without her being qualified in any way. At the time I thought it wasn't a big issue. I was wrong.

Reflections:

- Who would you confidently say constitute your 'personal base'? Why?

- And your 'professional base'—is yours sufficient for what you do?

Chapter 13

The Need to Upskill in the face of Diversity
Span —Is Number 8 wire the answer?

This is one of my favourite lines from the poem 'If' by Rudyard Kipling: "To meet Triumph and Disaster and treat those two imposters the same."

Success can be hard at times.

We know that failure is hard, we are programmed for that from early childhood.

But success? As it impacted some of our members, I also learned that it can be a beast. They were ending up in places that were unpredictable, and their personal base was not yet developed for managing that unpredictability.

At one meeting I remember one member had just received a grant from a government agency for $12m for research and development on an export project. He was ecstatic and was sharing all the things they were planning to undertake. Four months later when we caught up next, he was almost unrecognisable. He was frazzled and suffering from burnout. The human resources hadn't been built ahead of the investment.

It's easy to get things started for many people, but harvesting the rewards takes a different skill set and focus. It's a very common theme across our entire journey. Not being prepared for success. Not having the other skills ready down the line. That's a Kiwi issue I believe that comes from what we call the 'number 8 wire' syndrome, originating from when we were a nation of farmers—you can fix anything with a piece of number 8 wire. As things become more complex, the number 8 wire methodology of doing things on the smell of an oily rag, falls over all too quickly.

Our diversity of the membership was now expanding due to the successful experiment with the school principal, and I was needing to learn more subtle skills as that happened. This is ongoing work for me even today. Diversity sounds easy, but it takes a broad set of skills and attitude to enable inclusivity. As the saying goes, "It's one thing to be invited to the party. It's another to be allowed to sing and dance at it."

Oh, there were snags. One of them was learning about the many and subtle forms of addiction. I learned the hard way when a host was in the process of receiving feedback from the team and blew up, becoming highly distressed. The session needed to be brought to a close abruptly; I took the host away to try and settle things down, which we did eventually. I could not fathom what had triggered this outburst. The business was doing reasonably well, and the feedback was delivered with care as we always try to accomplish.

After a while the host asked for a drink, which in the circumstances I was willing to oblige, and to my amazement he nearly skulled a bottle of Chardonnay and proceeded to open another. I started to ask a few more questions and a darker picture emerged.

Thankfully, I wasn't by myself anymore and had others to talk this through with, otherwise this incident would have eaten me up. In conversation, and some confidential probing, I found out our host was indeed an alcoholic. This set me off on a mission of research to understand more, and one conclusion was that our CQ process was not what they needed, and we were not qualified to deal with such addictions.

I want to say at this point that some of the most well-developed people we have worked with over the years have been reformed addicts. The depths they have been to and then to rise again after help is one of the most admirable things I have experienced. The other thing is that I had no idea how many addictions there are, and I'm sure we have only scratched the surface.

I think I will stop here before I write something I'm out of my depth to fully understand.

After this incident, I thought, *Why don't we ask people before they join if they are addicts or have psychological issues that we should know about?* However, it was gently pointed out to me (by a reformed addict) this wasn't very mana-enhancing, and that maybe we just develop the skills to deal with this as each case arose. This is what we have tried to do.

On being a CQ team member

Around this time it was also pointed out to me that I should join one of our teams as an active member. The person who suggested this was a pain in the arse. And this too was another learning for me at this stage. Sometimes the biggest pain in the arse can give you the most valuable information, if you can hear it. It's not easy, but something on which I'm continually working.

So I joined our newest group at the time of its inception as a member and have got to say, without this team, the Collective Intelligence business would not exist today.

Our facilitator was Sue Johnston, who at the time (and still today, actually) was on a steep learning curve in her career on which I was lucky enough to be swept up. Sue was the first person to teach me about feedback. It was gold.

Here's how this unfolded. Our process is to ask for written feedback after each meeting. It's voluntary. The source is not confidential, and we share it with the facilitator. One day I was the facilitator that got rubbish feedback. I was seriously pissed: *They didn't know. They were wrong. They had no idea of the back story, or how hard I had worked to get this meeting together—blah blah blah.*

So I called Sue. She said, "Harv, it's only information. Sometimes it's useful, sometimes it's not, but what is there for you to learn?".

Fuck off, I thought, *they're still wrong.* Have I mentioned I'm a stunning sulker? Sue persisted and worked with me over months helping me to not only stop sulking but learning how to harvest the goodness that lay within the feedback. Thankfully she helped me with this, because I was destined for some very rich feedback in the not-too-distant future.

Listening to win

I also started practicing giving feedback. In my opinion, developing this skill of both giving and receiving feedback (information) is one of the most groundbreaking skills a person can obtain. It can create whole new pathways.

Sue was also training to certify for some new programs and would use me as a guinea pig to become certified. For me it was the gift of development that I may not have received otherwise. One of these was from some new woman called Brené Brown from Texas. I was immediately struck at just how practical and accessible her work was, all based on extensive research. Accessibility is a hallmark. I think is so important in anyone's work. It's often overlooked.

Of course Brené Brown is now world-famous, but back then not so much. Sue had the great pleasure of training directly with Brown in Australia, which, because of Brown's now fame, I don't think would be possible today. The training Sue gave me was all about building my personal base of emotional intelligence, which at the time I knew was a privilege and as time has gone by, that appreciation has grown. Reading Brené Brown's books is a great start, but actually doing the training is where the growth happens.

'Listening to win' was one of the most important lessons for me to learn from Sue's training. Both to catch myself doing it and observing it in others. I have lent on this training dozens of times with great effect.

By now we had more members who were not solely commerce focused, and it was adding to the expanding horizons of everyone concerned. There is absolutely nothing like getting behind the scenes of an enterprise to see how things really work.

For example, here's a sequence we had in play in one week. One CQ team was on a farm on Mahia Peninsula, while another was looking at a business that serviced the electronics of the drive-in system at Burger King on Auckland's North Shore. The next was in Wellington understanding the complexity of bureaucracy of central government and another was in Christchurch with the principal of a secondary school. We were stretching and humming along!

One day Jane had an idea. She said, "One of my daughters has a boyfriend who has a new business in eco housing. He's out on his own doing excellent work and would benefit from being in a Collective Intelligence team, but he can't afford it. Why don't we create a scholarship program?"

So we had a go.

More diversity

The first recipient was a young man from the Manawatū by the name of James McCarthy. (I'm literally sitting next to him at The Grid in Britomart using one of his spare desks, right now. Love this kind of co-incidence).

James was introduced to us by a third party who thought we could help him with his board makeup. We couldn't at the time, but after speaking with him we thought to offer him a scholarship. After much questioning, he accepted.

James was 24 years old, and I wondered how this experiment was going to work. He was by far the youngest person we had worked with at that point—was he going to fit in?

I was facilitating the team he joined and both of us were a little nervous when he came to the first meeting. I left him till the end of the first afternoon to fully introduce himself so he could first get the gist of the scene.

His first full sentence was gold: "Well, I'm not as fucked up as you lot are."

The team roared with laughter, and responded almost in unison, "Give it time James, give it time."

James was a co-founder of an IT company called Spider Tracks who tracked planes around the globe. He had multiple shareholders and investors in the company. The future was looking bright.

Four months later when the team met again, James' life was well fucked up. He sat down at the meeting and stated he was going to chuck it in, head off to Europe and get a job with a multinational company. His co-founders were causing strife, and he wanted out.

The team listened intently, drawing out the pain the young man was feeling. No sympathy, just well-crafted questions.

Then a question from a 56-year-old CEO of a listed company comes in from left field. "Why don't you buy the shares from that troublesome shareholder, and take the vacant CEO position?"

James responded immediately, "I'm only 24 and don't know how to be a CEO."

"Well, neither do I James, but that doesn't stop me."

James just sat in silence, as did everyone else.

Then: "So what do I need to be as a CEO?" And the conversation started from there.

The personal insecurity, the lack of knowing what to do, the inexperience, the unknown.

"Lead, James, lead. You can do it."

"Be bold and vulnerable," someone said.

"Bring them along the journey with you," another said.

"No one knows all the answers, and nor should they or you," they added.

These were the comments and conversations that went on, not just for that meeting, but for years to come.

The fascinating thing is that James trusted his Collective Intelligence team more than his own judgement. That is not an isolated occurrence.

The beauty of our work is that we work with members for years as they evolve. It was a rocky ride for James, and yet patching into his team every four months was highly valuable for him and his CQ team who were always ready to support.

His language and behaviour changed as he grew into his potential from a sometimes-awkward leader of his hi-tech company to a highly successful CEO. His language and behaviour were now international, and he travelled to the company's markets, building a team offshore as well as in Aotearoa New Zealand. He shifted the business from the Manawatū to Auckland in the hunt for more skilled labour.

In time, James hosted his team in Auckland and we got a good chance to get under the hood of Spider Tracks. Technically and personnel wise, the company was doing well. James reflected that the growth in the USA was booming, but he didn't think he felt comfortable travelling there at times. The team felt something was amiss, but couldn't put their finger on it, and one of them even stated that he thought they didn't have the full picture. James responded that everything relevant had been shared. All in all it was a very successful Host Day.

Now, we have a mantra today at Collective Intelligence—"The Issue is never the Issue".

A few weeks before the team was to meet next, I was putting the agenda together and I got a call from James. He was drunk. It was about 6pm. Something was up.

"Harv, I need to share something with you."

I said, "Sure."

"Harv… I'm gay."

"Oh. Okay. Great." (I'm so eloquent at these times.)

James was part sobbing and part laughing. It was all very intense, I told him that I was very honoured he was telling me and scrambled not to break the connection that was happening. He then said, "I don't know if I should tell the team."

I laughed and said, "Well I'm putting the agenda together as we're speaking, and I'll put it in to start the day off."

I wasn't sure if he was choking or just gurgling. He was choking as it turned out. "I'm not sure."

"Are you coming out or not?"

"I'm coming out!"

"Right, well here's what I'm putting on the agenda: *And now for something completely different!* If you change your mind, then I can put something else in its place."

We talked some more, and he said his main fear was that there was an older chap in the team who was quite conservative and from the Catholic faith. He was concerned he may get a rather negative response from him.

I said, "Well I'll ring him prior, and if he's got any negativity to this, I will deal with that—and let you know the outcome."

I duly rang this bloke and the response was hilarious. He said, "I couldn't care less and what are you really ringing for?"

So that hurdle was dealt with.

The day arrived and the team filed into the meeting room, and I got a few comments of intrigue about the *And now for something completely different!* item on the agenda. Then James arrived and he was white as a ghost. Oh my God. At that point I had never felt such an intense sense of compassion for a CQ member. So I thought, *Best get this underway as soon as possible.*

"James, you have something to share with the team."

Quiet—fidgeting—deep breath, "I'm gay."

It was stunning to observe the responses—which were all different.

"You are joking."

"Oh okay. Didn't see that coming."

"Argh, wondered what we were missing!"

And one other, which was delightful. A young woman in the team, from the next generation of scholarship recipients, had admired James from afar but had never gotten any vibes back. She sat there with a bemused smile on her face.

After 30 minutes of Q and A we were ready to move on, which the older fella had been waiting for impatiently. That night over dinner we all celebrated. What a privilege to be part of this momentous moment.

James became what was always evident to us—a leader of people who was reflective, inclusive, with an emotional intelligence that meant people wanted to be around him.

And then James got so bloody good at leadership, he retired at 34 years of age by bringing through a successor as the CEO. Bastard!

Retirement for James lasted all of eight months before he created his next start-up, Cradle, which he works on full time today.

What's been really cool for our relationship with James is that we have been able to work with no less than a dozen of his leadership team over the past 13 years. As a result, James has two successful businesses under his belt, while developing the next generation of leaders at the same time.

At Collective Intelligence, we are all about developing the next generation of leaders the world actually needs.

This afternoon I got to hear where his life is at, happily married and wanting to have kids. James McCarthy, you were the most amazing trailblazer for our scholarship program in which we have gone on to develop dozens of young professionals as young as 19 years that has endured to this day. Thank you for your participation and inspiration.

Reflections:

- When was the last time you shared something really personal about yourself?

- How did this affect you? What did you learn?

- What were your impressions from others' responses?

Chapter 14

Doing Business for the Sake of Shareholder Returns Only is One Way to Fuck the Planet Quickly — How will future generations have the environment they can enjoy?

"What is a social entrepreneur?" I whisper to the person next to me.

"I will explain later, Harv."

"Okay."

So I sat through the rest of this baffling TED Talk in central Wellington listening to an English fella who seemed to know what he was about. *Why social enterprise is a good idea* was the title of the talk. It seemed like a good idea.

I had never heard these terms before. Social enterprise. Social entrepreneur. Sounded a bit wankerish, but also compelling at the same time. Odd mix, right!

There was another TED Talk all about crowdfunding. This was another mind bender. I was listening to this smart, confident young woman with an odd accent, thinking *Cool idea*—but I could not for the life of me have repeated a word from the talk, such was the foreignness of the topic to my world view at the time.

There were other great speakers, but they didn't grab my attention like these two did.

So at the end of the session, I stuck around and cornered these two speakers at separate intervals. Some of you reading will have guessed I had been listening to Alex Hannant, and then Anna Guenther. Both were engaging and generous in explaining further what they were working on.

Alex was the CEO of the Hikurangi Trust, which was like a mother ship for social enterprises in Aotearoa New Zealand, later to become Ākina (which means 'To challenge, to encourage, or urge onwards'). Anna had founded PledgeMe which has been a hero of crowdfunding in Aotearoa New Zealand ever since.

I was convinced I wanted them as members of Collective Intelligence to broaden our diversity base at the time. Anna qualified as a scholarship recipient at the time so that was easy, and we found a way to get Alex started even though Hikurangi were not flush with funds.

These two opened up so many pathways for Collective Intelligence and have had a big impact on our development ever since. Anna has taught me to be braver in my convictions by watching her champion a number of wonderful initiatives.

Alex has a brain that thinks in systems and patterns I don't even know exist, and it's fascinating watching him process his thoughts while he twirled his finger in his left forelock of hair. Then comes a torrent of thoughts that cascade in a rush of energetic words that I think makes sense. I've never told him I generally have no fucken idea what he's saying—but the delivery is always impressive.

Most of all, it was a delight to meet people who gave enough of a fuck to try and change the world. I wasn't alone. It helped me understand what I was trying to create without actually knowing it—a social enterprise of sorts—although we are considered by some as being too capitalistic to be a social enterprise. That's bollocks, in my opinion.

Alex produced another bonus one day when he said he had joined a board in Australia called B Lab. He told me I should look into it, as I would really like the people involved. Of course he was referring to the B Corp movement which is all about building commercial companies that do more good than harm.

I was immediately interested and learnt it was a growing global movement but very new to Aotearoa New Zealand with only about nine companies accredited at the time. The more I looked into it the more I thought we would fly in. Everyone said it was hard, but we were special. So we began the process of accreditation—where you only need to get a 40 percent pass mark to become accredited. 80 marks from a possible 200. Easy.

We had put an intern onto the case and allowed him to guide us through the process. He had come back and said, "All done—I think you will get 120 points." And I believed him. What a dick.

This was the same time that Ākina was hosting the World Social Enterprise forum in Christchurch in 2017. Flash *as*. Alex was in his element—and I have to say I felt very proud of his huge achievement with the help of an epic team. Meanwhile I'm telling the people from around the world we had gone through the B Corp assessment and smashed the target—looking at a score of around 120. Maybe more.

When it came to the assessment, we found out we had 74.5 points. A humbling moment. Yes, it's very hard to get. We pulled out all the stops and finally climbed to 84.5 with a big sigh.

Today there are 165 B Corps in Aotearoa New Zealand who are not waiting for government directives; they are proactively advancing towards reducing carbon emissions, minimising waste, and ensuring fair labour practices. It's very cool.

But I have got to stress—they are not perfect. B Corps are always a work in progress and development. It's something I love about the movement.

As I have written earlier, of being so proud of my family doing good while doing the business—relating to the family continuing to build the Tui Brewery tower despite the effects of the depression in 1931.

What resonated so strongly with me is that growing up I was surrounded by two local businesses which had expanded rapidly in my youth.

The first was the Tui Brewery which was bought by Dominion Breweries (DB) in 1969 and expanded and upgraded rapidly in 1971-2 with a new brewing facility and bottling hall.

The other was the amalgamation of many of the local cheese factories into one larger company, called the Tui Milk Products Company (they were obviously short of original names back then).

So at one end of our wee farm, Te Kowhai, was the Tui Brewery—and at the other, a large cheese making plant, the Tui Cheese Company.

It was all very exciting and progressive.

Both now needed to develop effluent plants to process the considerable wash that was generated.

So the Brewery built a state-of-the-art European-designed waste treatment plant. Oh it was flash as! It had big paddles that circulated the brown waste in a big oval canal, separating the gunk from the liquid that would be distributed into the Mangatainoka river (the 'Toki') cleaner than the river water that was already there. That was the spin anyway. It was so flash that no one in Aotearoa New Zealand seemed to be able to get the thing to work.

The river soon flows into the Manawatū river about five kilometres downstream, as do four other river systems flowing from both the east and west. The outlet into the Toki from this European-designed effluent plant system was just below our house. I would wander down and watch brown liquid flowing steadily into the river, with a slipstream of brown slime sticking to the willow trees on the banks of the river. It didn't look good to my 12-year-old eyes. This trail of slime lasted about a kilometre in the late winter of 1972 while there was good flow in the river. This of course was the tip of the iceberg.

The summer of 1972/73 in North Wairarapa was a drought to be remembered. It started in early December and didn't let up until late March. By early December I noticed the brown trout in the river were becoming lethargic. It was odd as they were normally incredibly shy and sensitive fish, and very hard to get near, but now I could corner them in a backwash and nearly catch them with my bare hands. By January, I could catch them. They were terrible to eat as the taste was just awful, and they had no condition on them.

What transpired was that the trout just didn't have enough oxygen in the water, and they were literally suffocating. Many had fled upstream from the brewery outlet, but many remained in the kilometres of river downstream.

One afternoon I was walking along the riverbank and thought I spied an eel in midstream. It was not very big, and it was unusual to spot them out in the open in full view and sunlight. So I waded in for a closer look, and was confused to find it wasn't an eel at all, but a lamprey. I had never seen a live lamprey before because they are so shy. They look like an eel, but don't have a mouth with teeth—rather a round sucker type mouth which allows them to attach to large fish in the sea when they migrate out of the rivers.

This lamprey looked sick with bruises on it. So I caught it with my hands and took it home alive to put in my eel tank I had developed out of an old bath where I kept a few of my slimy pets. Then I set off to raise the alarm, telling my father I had caught a lamprey. He had never seen a live one either, so I fished him out of the old bath.

"He looks crook," says Bill, "like the trout I have been catching." Yep, just like the trout.

Back then we didn't have the Department of Conservation; we had some local outfit. So my dad Bill tells me to ring them and tell them about the lamprey.

So, as instructed, I ring the local conservation outfit, and the fella tells me it was a bad thing to catch them as they are so rare and shy. (Adults on a bad day are such dicks). "Yes" I said, "I know that (you dick), but this one's crook because of the water, and all the slime growing on the rocks in the river."

"Put it back," says the adult from the local outfit. "It's just the drought." So I did, in a pool near the house, and went down to see how it was the next day. It was lying there, upside down, dead. Had my interference killed it? Maybe.

So my curiosity got the better of me and I went off looking for any others—and bingo, found two more dying lamprey. So I rang the adult up again, and this time got his interest.

He would look into it, he said. He came and took some samples, which indicated yes, the water was indeed low on oxygen, and high on bad stuff.

Then precisely nothing happened and life went on, and I went off to start at Rathkeale College.

However, there was an indelible imprint in my subconscious.

The subtle environmental carnage continued for years to come with the Tui Brewery, its wonderful advertising glitz of the Tui Girls and 'Yeah, Right' slogan masking what was really happening in real life, out-of-sight, at the brewery.

Dominion Brewery finally got the European-designed effluent canals working in a moderate fashion: the effluent into the river wasn't brown any more. Instead, they were irrigating the brown stuff onto our farm! To them it was seen as free fertiliser, but in reality, it was spread way too thick to break down into the soil between irrigations, and it was causing issues of ponding and anaerobic puddles. It seemed the whole waste disposal gig was a low cost afterthought that was just a nuisance to management.

What was evident from the outset with DB's buy-out in 1969 was it was about volume of beer sold, and not much else. There was little to know of regarding history or the whakapapa of the place of Mangatainoka.

The artesian water that lay beneath the area, with the wonderful taste? Well, if you build a European designed concrete effluent canal on top of it, in a few years and several earthquakes later, it begins to leak. Slowly enough that no one notices.

That is until I got a call from the head chemist at the Tui Brewery around 1985. He asked if we could meet confidentially somewhere quiet. I was intrigued. I'm not going to mention his name. He asked if we were drinking the artesian water at home at all. I said, "Only when the water tank was low."

He gave a big sigh and said, "Don't ever drink the water again if you are planning to start a family." (I was married at this time and starting a family was on the horizon).

He said with a very sad voice, "I'm sorry to say the artesian water is now contaminated with nitrates."

"So what happens if we do drink it," I asked.

"A chance of a blue baby, and other health issues."

I had never heard of this before. I was bewildered. Our beautiful ancient water was contaminated.

"How did this happen?"

"Our effluent canal has been leaking, and it's the source of the contamination."

I felt numb. And angry. He also thought it may be related to the intensification of the dairy herds in the area as well, but it was too early to be sure.

He went on to say that they were about to start building a huge tank behind the brewery to store the water from the well. The tank was to try and get the nitrates out of the water before they used it to make the beer.

He asked me to not say anything to anyone about this. They were going to get this sorted as quickly as possible.

The next day they indeed brought in the heavy machinery to build a platform for this massive tank.

My mother was watching proceedings from the kitchen window. It was mid-morning when she realised they were cutting down the oak trees planted behind the Brewery in 1920 for every local that was killed in the First World War. Twelve in total. Two were my great uncles.

Lois jumped in the car in her apron and drove down to confront the contractors, but to no avail. Bill and I went down at lunch time. Even the head brewers who we knew well were not interested in our protests. Deaf ears. They needed a new tank no matter what. It was all happening so fast and there was a lot of tension in the air.

By nightfall all the beautiful memorial oak trees were cut down. We all sat and cried for this invasive and personal loss. Progress be damned. My mother tried swearing—it just didn't come out right, and Bill and I both laughed. It felt good to laugh at least.

Since then, I have never knowingly drunk Tui beer.

Meanwhile, at the other end of the farm, the pollution was more obvious. The Tui Dairy company was sending raw whey (by-product of making cheese) down a man-made channel into the stoney creek that flowed through our farm. By February, you could literally walk on top of the skin of dried whey floating about the water. Fuck, it stunk.

They thought that irrigating the whey onto our alluvial paddocks would be a better resolution to the problem. Which it sort of was, for a while. But the whey would be flowing from August and the paddocks were still waterlogged at this point, and no good to irrigate.

So they put a pipe in that let the whey out into the stoney creek further downstream so nobody could see the pollution—apart from us, that is. Oh, and where did the stoney creek flow into? Yep, the Mangatainoka river.

Even the irrigation was a problem because it was fouling up the soil structure and our free-draining soils became gluggy. A good friend and neighbour at the time, who was a zoologist, suggested I could introduce a native worm which creates a permanent burrow to about a metre (cool eh) that may help with deep aeration. So off we go to have a look at the environment.

We both stood in front of a moving irrigator and witnessed thousands upon thousands of worms come out of their burrows in the middle of the day and moving to get out of the way of the stream of whey. The whey also contained caustic soda from the wash-up process at the factory—the worms knew what they were doing!

I'm retelling these two stories because the impact they had on me was deep and hasn't diminished with time.

Doing business for the sake of shareholder returns only is one way to fuck the planet, and quickly.

So when B Corp crossed my path, it was like I had been waiting for this to happen for half my life. It was a no brainer to certify.

Reflections:

- This chapter is all about our impact on the environment. What's been your personal contribution to help saving our planet for future generfations?

Chapter 15

Becoming Conscious — Outliers are curious, ambitious, authentic and often complex

"Harv, I see you are putting up the annual membership for Collective Intelligence. I'm phoning to say I'm not getting any value from my team and am going to pull out."

"Richard, you wouldn't get any value out of your team even if it was free!"

"Why is that?" he said.

"Because you're not doing any work between the meetings. Your team is frustrated because you bring the same issues to the table every bloody meeting and don't actually do anything about them. So no wonder you are not getting any value."

Richard took this well, and applied himself and became an excellent member for the next six years, making huge strides in his life.

The biggest impacts for me though were these:

- Why were some CQ members gaining so much value from our process and others weren't?
- What was the difference between these two groups?

After six years of facilitating teams, I was gaining enough maturity and space to begin reflecting on the big question.

When an experience is very new to you, the senses are full, taking in all the first-time sights and sounds. There's also a whole bunch of stuff you don't see. Sportspeople express this when competing on a big stage for the first time, often saying how everything moves fast and in a blur. The game is over before they know it. As they get more attuned to this big stage, they are able to play the game and notice the crowd and surroundings. They take in more of the theatre in which they are playing. That's consciousness coming into play.

If you have ever walked a beach on the hunt for and picking up litter, it's hard to walk a beach again and not see the litter and pick it up. That's consciousness.

Becoming aware of your own emotions in real time, and why those emotions are in play is also a sign of consciousness.

I was becoming conscious about our range of members and in particular a group of outliers, and one outlier stood out from even that group. He intrigued me, in that he had achieved so much in his personal and professional life, yet here he was fully engaged in one of our Collective Intelligence teams giving and receiving so much goodness.

Outliers are always a gift; you can learn so much from them. We had already had an outlier team and learnt so much from them.

So I went back to work and studied what this outlier chap had that some others didn't.

It took about six months of reflection. Slowly the fog lifted, and I could see the attributes he possessed that others didn't. It seems so obvious now. There are three attributes—curiosity, ambition and authenticity.

Curiosity

He had that in spades. He would look for the things that were not obvious. He'd listen intently for the answer that was not crystal clear and dig a bit more. Curiosity is a wonderful thing—if you are brave enough to use it well. Because if you are truly curious, you are going to uncover things that are uncomfortable at best, and scary at worst.

Being curious about others is super important to be a Collective Intelligence member, because we are not about putting like-minded people together.

Collective Intelligence curates teams of like-hearted people instead.

We expect our members to disagree with each other—and harness what flows from that space.

Ambition

This chap was ambitious about making a difference in the world. He was an introvert, but would push the boat out when needed and front crowds if that was going to make a difference to a good cause.

He fully understood he was the biggest limitation in his own life, and that he needed to work on himself to not get in the way of what he was capable.

This type of personal ambition gives an individual the ability to keep developing even when it's hurting. A bit like an athlete training—nothing happens until the pain gets to a seven out of 10. It's what they do at that pain point that determines the fitness level they achieve.

He could push through the discomfort to gain a new level of whatever he was seeking.

To facilitate him was challenging and a gift. There were always surprises.

He wasn't interested in fame or fortune. He was interested in leaving the world a better place than he had found it.

Authenticity

This was the strongest of the three attributes I zeroed in on. The guts to be yourself. This chap with all he had achieved, could turn up, and be so vulnerable with his team. He sought assistance with what he needed to work on.

He had led a tumultuous life in his earlier years and had overcome formidable personal challenges along the way. He still bore some of the scars from that time. Yet he never shied away from what was really going on.

Brené Brown talks of armour. It's the shield people create to protect themselves from who they really are. It's so hard to facilitate, communicate, or live with armoured people, as you just can't connect with them—you often can't get past the armour.

This chap was the opposite of that.

Having a baseline of competence in the CQ team members helps as well—but I have almost assumed this is a given these days.

Curious. Ambitious. Authentic. These attributes *all* fluctuate. They are not constant. They rise and fall. Even your competence level should be rising and falling, because it's a sign you are developing.

Unfortunately, since I first focussed on authenticity, it has become one of those buzz words. I hear people say, "I want to be my most authentic self all of the time". I often wonder if some of the buzzers actually know what authenticity is or how brave you need to be to try that.

These are the attributes we look for today in our members, because when you have a curated team of people with these attributes in a safe space, you can absolutely make sense of complexity.

Complexity

That's the next bit I was becoming conscious of—complexity. It's a thing that keeps growing in the world and yet people are less able to recognise or cope with complexity than ever before.

I see more and more people wanting simple answers to complexity in order to feel less afraid. Enough Americans will vote for a figure like Trump who simplifies complex issues helping voters to feel more secure in the world—in my opinion.

I've been on a Facebook group for the past twelve months called Geoengineering. They are looking at the clouds reporting on chemtrails being sprayed out by planes as they fly across the country. Air New Zealand, the New Zealand Air Force and private planes are apparently spraying chemicals daily to change the weather to suppress us all. It's being conducted by 'Them', 'They'—I never could find out exactly who.

Recently I got kicked off Geoengineering for asking some questions about some of the posts that were being put up. Naughty, I know.

What I was intrigued to find out was, what was motivating 14,000 people to be part of this conspiracy Facebook group? I think it's to give some comfort in the face of climate change and loss of biodiversity which are complex issues. If 'They' stopped spraying us with chemtrails daily, we would be fine. Bonus point for these people is that we don't need to change anything in our own lives, as it's out of our control anyway. We can blame an invisible enemy, instead of having to take responsibility and action ourselves.

The next big learning opportunity was when our Māori membership grew and have now been one of the biggest influencers in our evolution. Without initially being conscious of it, we were utilising much of their culture already.

We fortunately began attracting young, smart Māori leaders who proudly championed their culture into our ecosystem. This enabled my world views to be challenged (albeit in a very gentle way). Riria Te Kanawa, her husband Che Wilson, and then Liana Poutu joined up at a similar time. They are all well-versed in their culture and were incredibly generous with their time to educate us on their ancestors' journeys. I was immediately struck by the fact that I had little idea of Aotearoa New Zealand's history.

I also gained an appreciation of the difficulty and time it took for Iwi to go through a Waitangi Tribunal settlement.

Fortunately, we had a facilitator at the time, Megan Rose, who encouraged me to attend a two-day Treaty education workshop run by Robert Consedine. The course was called 'Healing our History'—also the name of a book he wrote with his daughter Joanna Consedine.

It was a stunning two days, due to Consedine's experience with Treaty work over many years. He gave a global perspective of what was going on in the world when the Treaty was signed and did not make anyone feel embarrassed or vilified by the events that make up our shared history. I gained a far better perspective of how our country has been shaped, and came away not only enlightened, but with a new sense of personal identity.

I had no real understanding prior to this workshop of how little Iwi were being recompensed by the Crown (just 1 to 2 percent), for the land that had been confiscated in the mid-1800s. This really brought home to me the impact on Māori as a people. It was incredibly uncomfortable to examine and understand the effect colonisation has had on Iwi, hapū, and whānau. I started to understand why Dame Whina Cooper led the hikoi (a walk or march, and especially a protest march or parade), and why our jails are overly full of Māori.

I learnt that early colonial governments drafted land laws after land laws to try and break down Iwi, and to get a hold of the land needed to settle the one million immigrants shipped in over 60 years from 1840 to 1900. During that same period, the Māori population plummeted due to disease and the Land Wars.

I also came away feeling very proud of our country. While becoming more knowledgeable was uncomfortable, it was also comforting to gain perspective. It is also important for me to say that I am no authority on our history, but I am deeply interested.

What has intrigued me in working with Collective Intelligence teams over the years, is that whenever Māori members have brought their culture into the room, the experience for everyone deepens.

Māori understand the idea of 'collective intelligence' instinctively. It's how they operate.

I have witnessed Riana Manuel integrate the Matariki constellation model used in a meeting feedback process with stunning effectiveness. The use of karakia (Māori incantations and prayer used to invoke spiritual guidance and protection) can deepen the connection between members, and impromptu waiata (a Māori song usually commemorative of some important event) to celebrate. I am still clumsy when engaging with the Māori culture, but learning every day.

In 2024, there is still a huge amount of misunderstanding by many Pākehā of what Te Ao Māori is, and often a mistrust of the Treaty settlements where I hear comments like, "Will the settlements ever be finished?" and "When will Māori be satisfied?"

Bad news sells. And there is plenty of bad news when reporting on Māori issues. But what we have been able to learn at Collective Intelligence is how much good news there is to do with Māoridom.

Pākehā will need to find a way to get alongside Māori quickly or get left behind as the rise of the Māori culture, economy and leadership in indigenous affairs make them world leaders that other ethnicities look up to.

When you get close to others, you will learn you have more in common than not. It's a key driver of mine with our work at Collective Intelligence.

Reflections:

- This chapter introduces 'ambition' and 'complexity' and refocuses on 'authenticity' as key attributes of people who may be termed, 'outliers'—people who perhaps sound and behave a little differently. What's been your experience with those people you know who could be described as 'outliers'?

- How did this experience affect you? What did you learn?

- The chapter also introduces another aspect of diversity—Māori. If you're a Kiwi reading this, what has been the impact of the Māori culture on you, your team, your organisation? If you're not from Aotearoa New Zealand, what other 'cultural impacts' have you learnt from?

- Another key concept discussed here is 'consciousness'—becoming aware of your current environment and particularly own emotions in real time, and why those emotions are in play. The key here is 'in real time'—have you experienced this? When? If not, what would it take for you to do so, in a new experience?

Chapter 16

Accuracy of 'Feelings' is an Important Muscle to Grow — Being aware enough to express your feelings

"What's wrong with the bottled water, Harv? For goodness' sake, you're just being silly."

When challenged, I had no idea how to respond in the moment, and I thought I was making a mountain out of a molehill. However, I was feeling a little frustrated at the attitude of my old friends who were, like me, from privileged backgrounds.

We meet every year in October and take turns at organising the three days away to enjoy each other's company and tell tales of years gone by. This particular year the organisers had set up a wonderful meal with local chefs and local produce in a very cool setting. What could go wrong?

As we were eating dinner, some bottled water was placed in front of each of us. In my earlier life I would have just opened and drunk the water without a thought. Now though, it made me feel conscious of our unrecognised privilege where others, not so privileged, would be drinking tap water. I looked across at my wife Kate, who just shrugged her shoulders indicating she had no answer either.

So I got up and went to the nearby tap, trying not to draw attention. But it did, and it pissed our hostess for the evening off big time. That's when I got the challenge from our hostess: "What's wrong with the bottled water, Harv?"

Here's the thing. At that moment, two old friends were aggrieved over bottled water. Yes, we'd had a wine (or two) by this stage—which never helps—but I play that episode through my mind often because it symbolises to me the gaps that are occurring in the world.

How could I have handled that better?

My friends and I discussed it the next day, but to this day I have never felt heard or understood.

In this period of getting my head up and observing the world through a wider lens, it was fascinating to see what was previously hidden to me. However, there are a number of downsides to being more aware. Firstly, it's tiring. You get to see injustices and become frustrated with systems that are essentially built for the privileged. Secondly, for me anyway, it's a struggle not to call people out all the time for sexism, racism, and stuff like environmental negligence, which just pisses people off.

At that time, I hadn't built the capacity to call people out with words that are inclusive and helps build their own capacity. This is something I'm still working on.

Being the founder of Collective Intelligence has given me the profound privilege of looking into so many world views and industries. It's one of the motivations to write this book—to share some of those insights. Plus I have been awarded an Edmund Hillary Fellowship recently, which exposes me to more change makers from across the globe.

The impact of both of these ecosystems has changed me.

Previously in my life I have not been able to recognise the signs of social change as they are happening. Normally the change is pointed out after, and I'm like, *Oh yeah, I can see that in hindsight.* Hindsight is easy.

So I've surprised myself, when I start to notice social changes as they are happening and also witnessing their impact. And I now feel a sense of responsibility to raise the alarm when it's warranted.

Here's one big issue I am seeing: The Great White Male (GWM) is struggling to cope with the complex and changing world we live in, and there is carnage already.

In some way, I feel for these previous dominants as they struggle to adjust to the emerging world, where status and money are not as respected as collaboration.

Here's a reality check for the GWM.

The largest demographic group in the workforce the world has ever experienced are called Millennials. And Millennials are now in 23 percent of all leadership roles.

Most corporate and social structures have been designed by men, which often favour men—often unconsciously.

Women are determined to gain gender equality—and making huge inroads.

Māori are working their tails off to make up for lost opportunities caused by colonisation.

That's Aotearoa New Zealand. I daresay it's similar elsewhere.

All of these are having a direct effect on The Great White Male.

As Bob Dylan would say, "The times they are a changin'".

Sitting in the heart of a growing diverse community that is Collective Intelligence, I have witnessed the group that is struggling the most with the changing scene in our society, are the white males aged 45 years and above.

It's like watching a marathon race, where a runner is passed late in the race and just can't change tempo to keep up. And it's agonising to watch. And it's worse if you're the runner being passed. Ironically, men started this marathon early, and with better shoes (this only illustrates how hard women and Māori have worked).

So what have I specifically observed? Following are some examples.

Watching a late 50s bloke struggle with being challenged by a 30-something-year-old female, and not knowing how to respond, so resorting to bullying. *And* thought that was okay.

A male CEO asking for more people like him to come into his Collective Intelligence team, because he didn't see value in the diversity. When we pointed out this was not about like-mindedness, he was baffled.

Introducing an accomplished young Māori woman into an existing Collective intelligence team and having three older white men question the value of her contribution. They simply did not get it. And still don't. And they left.

A GWM didn't want to make the effort to attend a Collective Intelligence host meeting because he couldn't see what was in it for him. Recently, another GWM couldn't be bothered travelling to the lower South Island for a young woman's Host Day.

I have witnessed a good bloke leave a senior corporate position, and within seven years, move backwards three times, not realising he was not the formidable corporate bloke anymore.

Another chap from a rural background ringing me, complaining that the women in his team were not respecting his viewpoint on a number of issues. I asked if he had asked them why—the answer was, no, he hadn't. I suggested that he bring it up with them, which he still hasn't. His female facilitator rang him to discuss, left a message, and he didn't reply.

Another 50-something man lost his job, as he was unable to work for a 30-something female boss. He has vanished from all communication and will not engage with me.

I could go on, but this is painting the picture of what we have experienced. It's the last two points that concern me the most. When the world pushes in on these males, and they disappear from engagement—what then? This is the tip of the iceberg—and these men are everywhere, and hurting.

I heard a great quote recently from a knowledgeable chap Brendan Kelly, formerly Deputy Chief Executive Officer/Chief Information Officer from the Tertiary Education Commission. He made a very sage comment: "We are all four bad choices away from being unemployable." Spooky, but I think very accurate. My concern is that one particular demographic is making more poor choices than the rest combined.

The other observation is the bewilderment by the GWMs around the call for diversity on governance boards. I even heard one blurt out at a meeting, "Don't forget the wonderful experience we bring to the table." Experience in what? Bullying and domination?

Enough of the beat up. What to do about this?

A National Federation of Men? Possibly. The big issue is that the people who need the most assistance are not seeing that it's an issue until it affects them negatively—and then it seems too late. They go into fight or flight mode, and it's a long way back from there.

So to all you Great White Males—collaboration is here to stay. The days of dominating to get your point across are vanishing. So what skills are you going to develop to replace these? It will be fun and rewarding, if you're courageous enough to take up the challenge.

We grew up in a generation where white men ruled the roost. There were two key messages that were running strongly through our society about men in those days.

- Status matters, and you get status in Aotearoa New Zealand from being good at sport (particularly rugby) or having enough wealth to provide for your family.
- Don't show weakness—of any kind—ever. Big boys don't cry.

So unless you grew up with very enlightened parents, the script that you built about yourself and who you are will have these two messages embedded in it. So, you worked hard, made sacrifices, pushed through, sucked it up and soldiered on. Your family could eat, holiday, and get a good education.

You built a reputation as a great farmer/accountant/lawyer/engineer. Your peers promoted you as a 'good bloke'. The world you excelled in taught you that the best way to lead people was the command-and-control way. You are/were making a wonderful life. You are doing your best. You have experienced struggles.

The saddest of all the examples I have left to last.

We had a member who was a younger GWM, who had taken over his father's business when he died. His father had a big reputation and the ego to match. He was larger than life and had built a modest but iconic business.

His son took this over in his late 20s and worked his butt off to build the business even bigger than his father ever did. But he never enjoyed the experience because he was always trying to show his dead father just how good he was. This carried on for about 12 years before he joined Collective Intelligence.

I knew he was going to be a challenge and was hesitant to take him on, but the person who put him forward was a trusted member who told me the young guy needed help. So we took him on. We set up a three-year project just for him to see if we could make progress. I put him in a very strong team in the hope he would respond.

I remember asking him how he felt one day. He told me what he was thinking. I said, "No, not thinking—feeling. What are you feeling?". He had to Google what feelings were. He didn't know how he was feeling, ever.

His armour was immaculate. His dress sense was epic. He drank himself into oblivion often (I know we don't work with addicts—it was a favour). He would turn up on time and always look as if he had it together.

The call came on a Friday night from his good mate to say he had died in the early hours of Friday morning in his bed, choking on his vomit. I felt hollow and sad and frustrated.

I sought some counselling for that from one of our CQ members operating in the mental health sector. When I described the events, she smiled and said, "Don't fret Harv. You were never going to help him. We can't help him. AA couldn't help him. He's what we call 'terminally unique', in that they think they are so special they could kick the addiction at any point they chose to."

That was a wakeup call.

As I said earlier—being conscious can be tiring.

Final word on this subject. Learn to communicate as clearly and accurately as possible:

- If you are 'sad', say it,
- If you are 'scared', say it,
- If you are 'joyful', give that a go as well.

The more accurate you are, the better. 'Accuracy' is an important muscle to grow. You need to express how the fuck you are feeling.

Reflections:

- How comfortable (or uncomfortable) are you in expressing your feelings in the moment?

- If uncomfortable, what stops or hinders you from expressing your feelings?

- When you're experiencing some strong feelings about the situation and how it may be affecting you, it could be useful to start with, "I'm feeling …". Worth trying.

Chapter 17

Paradigm Shifts — Through honest and sincere feedback comes a paradigm shift

I got a text early one year from a wonderful member, Fee Webby, with a photo from a page in a book she had been given for Christmas. It had a note which said, "Read this. It's talking about your work. Literally."

I ordered this book and read it in two sittings with green marker spread all through it. Rebel Ideas by Matthew Syed was a bolt out of the blue. Here was someone from across the other side of the globe, writing about his experience and effectiveness of diverse teams.

I have reread it in preparation for writing this book, learning yet more from the third read. It's wonderful to bask in another writer's views condoning your work.

Throughout the past 17 years, there have been many memorable moments where paradigms have been sat on their arse and these have left an indelible impression on me. This chapter is a collection of ten of these moments.

1. Live your values

There is one Host Day that was one out of the box. It was unique because it went from zero to full throttle in about three hours. Fortunately, the host had the fortitude to handle the acceleration.

The host in question, Nick, was nearing the end of his professional career, and he was a very successful businessman involved in many enterprises around the globe. Nick was a modest, well-loved chap, in his late 50s. He had it all and was respected by the members of the team.

The younger members who revered him were wondering how they could actually add value to his life on this Host Day. Even though Nick had it all, he was still working hard in his finance business and had the drive of someone much younger.

It was very impressive.

Until we interviewed his children as part of the process. Then we learnt that Nick was not engaged with them. This was the deal he made with them a few years earlier: He had promised to ease up by now, but nothing was changing. The old habits were just that. They loved their father and knew just how much he had done for them. But they also felt life was running out and they just weren't able to connect with him.

Lunch arrived, and the team were a bit shaken—especially the younger ones. They had not expected this to be a big deal, but it was. How do we give this feedback?

I have always believed a Collective Intelligence team is always in the right place at the right time. It's uncanny. However, if you let the team choose where and when, then that's where the magic happens. As it happened, that day I was in the process of handing over the reins to the next facilitator Sue Johnson and asked her what she suggested we do with this situation over lunch.

With no hesitation, Sue said, "A values exercise with the whole team", which we included straight after the break. So the whole team and Nick got to start broad with their values, then narrowed them down one by one.

As it turned out, Nick's top value when he whittled it down to the single most important was family.

Big pause.

The reflection was profound. He was hit with a wave of emotion when he realised he was not honouring his number one value in life. Nick had a high EQ, so he was able to process this in real time with the team. In typical Nick style, he humbly thanked the team for the mirror being held up and committed to re-balancing his life.

The feedback from his family to the team a few months later was a beautiful heartfelt acknowledgement, saying they were enjoying having Nick fully in their lives for the first time in many years.

Never ignore the signals. You may not be living your values.

2. The power of feedback

"Harv, do you really want to increase the diversity of Collective Intelligence?"

"Of course I do."

"Well you might want to consider what it's like for this new young woman Lee, before you deliver a racist joke like that in future."

This was a conversation between Sarah Tocker and I while we were at Shoal Beach in Hawkes Bay, at the spiritual home of Collective Intelligence. We were in our bach, which Riana Manuel had named 'Tāmāta' (meaning a place to come together to share ideas and knowledge).

We had a new member, Lee, join the team. She was from the investment industry and super smart. And shy. And Asian. And I had made an off-hand Asian joke, thinking it was funny. The team had laughed at this seemingly light-hearted banter. Lee had just smiled.

When we had a quiet moment, Sarah had taken me aside and asked if I would like some feedback. I was taken aback at first. As I have said before, feedback is the lifeblood of growth, and here was a gift that Sarah was delivering with love.

But it was confronting and hard to take at the time. I felt embarrassed and ashamed of my arrogance and disregard for this guest.

I did apologise to Lee, and said I would try harder in the future to be more inclusive. It's work in progress.

As a privileged white male from the agricultural sector, I had never had feedback like this. In my previous life, I didn't need it. The whole system was designed for me.

I have drawn on this story for many years now. It's a wonderful reminder of how impactful feedback can be. It's a wonderful reminder also of how unrecognised privilege can be so blind to others. It's an ugly beast. It's a wonderful reminder too, that if you wish to grow diversity in your organisation, it's going to take time to grow your skill of being inclusive.

Thank you, Sarah!

3. Understanding others can initiate a massive paradigm shift

We were winding up the second day of a unique Host Day. Time was tight; people needed to get to the airport on time. We were in Ohakune, in the Central Plateau of the North Island, when our host Che Wilson, proclaimed he'd written a waiata of thanks to the team before the final wrap up.

It was beautiful. Soulful. What a gift.

Until he finished and the succinct roundup always done by each member went to pieces. I had tears and so much emotion to contend with—it was all very tricky on a limited time schedule.

Here is what unfolded.

At the beginning of the day, Che had outlined the fact that the average yearly Māori income per household was around $17,000 per annum, which blew our minds. Per household! That was well below the benefit levels that people could get from the government. He explained many of their people didn't want to receive benefits from the government, so they didn't apply for benefits like that. Also, Ohakune is in the Central Plateau—bloody cold in the winter –and many of the tribe lived in houses that were not well insulated, let alone heated.

Che was the CEO of his iwi, Ngati Rangi. We had been critiquing his performance in this role by interviewing his Chairman, some board members and then three uri (descendants) of the iwi.

The day was tracking well, until the three uri came to talk to us. All three had been subjected to tough lives in one way or another. Prison, violence, poverty and institutional failure. Understandably they were very nervous, and felt a bit intimidated by the team, even though I had tried to calm them earlier (sometimes I'm not very good at that). They told us about their lives and the struggles they had faced, which were all very poignant, very different and yet also very similar.

It was confronting to understand just how tough it was for underprivileged Māori. They weren't angry or complaining, and I think that was what made it even more confronting.

Then something wonderful happened.

They asked us why we were here. What were we about? So I told

149

them: To support Che's development and journey.

Oh my God, their faces lit up. They loved Che; that was obvious. Their response was totally spontaneous, and the shyness disappeared in a flash. I have tears in my eyes now remembering the moment.

They said they often worried about Che having to travel to Wellington for many years to negotiate for the iwi in preparation for the Waitangi Tribal settlement, which had not happened at this point. They worried about his welfare being in a hostile environment surrounded by Pākehā. But now they met us, and that we were here for him, made them feel that maybe not all Pākehā were heartless bastards.

This was delivered with humour, but also rather poignant, and definitely real. All the barriers were gone and they hugged us all as they left.

Then back to finish the day with the wrap-up and a waiata of thanks from Che.

In the team was a chap, born and bred in Christchurch. Great guy. Well, when it comes to the wrap-up, he's so tied up in emotion he can't speak. He's got tears rolling down his cheeks speechless. He wanted to say something, and so we all waited quietly. Then he said, "Until today I have never really talked with or engaged with Māori in my life, let alone heard their view of the world and the real challenges they face. I've been very judgemental of Māori and thought they were just lazy. I was so wrong."

Che smiled and nodded. The room was full of emotion and aroha (love).

Understanding others' lives breaks down so many barriers that we often don't even know exist. They are invisible. Yet these barriers can create divides that are so harmful.

4. A public paradigm shift

"Harv, I have pressure from colleagues to take the top job, but I have seen the way my previous boss worked, and I don't want that life. I want to have a family, *and* a life. Not just be this machine that is totally engulfed by the work."

"Well, why don't you do it your way? Do it differently? You don't have to copy the old style. Listen to your supporters but set the terms of how you want to function—and if they don't accept that, then move on."

"Hmmm. You are not the only one that expressed that view."

"We can help you through this stage, if you want."

This was a conversation that had its roots two years earlier.

My wife Kate was back from a stint in Samoa for work, where she had caught up with a colleague whom she respected very much. He had invited her to dinner with him and his wife. They got chatting about a number of things, and he asked what I did for a crust.

Kate went on to explain my work at Collective Intelligence, in which he became very interested, as he had a daughter whom he thought could do with some support. He went on to explain that she worked in Wellington and that her work schedule was long and gruelling at times. Being part of a diverse team would be just what she needed.

He gave the young woman's email to Kate. I followed up the next week, and I got no reply. I tried once more but to no avail. So I left it there. A few years later, a member named Fee Webby (from a previous chapter) emailed me and said she had just been visited at work by the same woman. She had got chatting and mentioned the benefit of being in one of our teams, and this young woman said she was keen.

Fee patched us in via email and I set up a time to meet her in Auckland next time I was up that way.

We met in a café in Newmarket one morning, and she was incredibly engaging, funny and we hit it off. Oh she was also liberal with the word 'fuck'. That was a surprise.

And we discussed her work situation.

This young woman joined a team soon after, but never really settled in as time commitments were always tight for her. Such is the life of a politician.

On March 15th, 2019, I watched this young woman on live television. By this point, she was our Prime Minister. Jacinda Ardern led the country as we reeled from the mosque attacks in Christchurch. To watch and hear her mature and heartfelt messages of, "This is not us" made me feel incredibly proud of our small nation.

I remember texting her around this time with, "You beauty", as I was at a loss to express anything more poignant.

Jacinda later also dealt with the White Island eruption in December the same year, while Covid-19 was finding its feet in Wuhan, China.

Her leadership through that first Covid 19 phase was textbook, leading to a landslide victory at the next election. I believe the Labour Party won more votes than were good for them. However, it was mostly due to her stunning leadership.

Some of you reading this now (especially if you are from Auckland) will be mumbling because of the extended lockdowns, the vaccination mandates, or some other grumble. Remember, that's mostly your bias at work, and we know by now what that does to your intelligence.

When Jacinda resigned from the job, I was so relieved. I cheered her choice to do this at this time. It had been the best of times and the worst of times for her tenure.

On social media there were some Great White Men saying some very, very, childish things on the evening of her resignation. I won't repeat them. So I tried calling them in. I asked, "If that was your daughter, would you be okay with saying these things?" Guess what—it worked. Not immediately. But it worked!

It will be interesting to see how the historians record Ardern's leadership influence on Aotearoa New Zealand. We can be very petty in this country and are very quick to take the tall poppies down.

Meanwhile she has done our nation a wonderful service in lifting our international profile that will endure for decades.

I wish I could say we had an influence on her leadership, but we can't. But she showed how powerful authenticity is when you are facing adversity. I look forward to catching up with her one day in the future and chewing the fat.

Never underestimate a determined woman.

5. A paradigm shift that could change the world

We have a tradition in CQ of new members giving their timeline—that is, their life's story.

One stands out above most.

Eva's life was rich and interesting, beginning in the UK and moving to Aotearoa New Zealand. She was obviously very creative and had a love of all things design. Eva talked about having a family, her first marriage not working out, and how she was now in a fabulous relationship with the love of her life Anne, whom she had known since they were teenagers.

Great timeline. However, the next two sentences from Eva were epic. She said, "So is everyone feeling comfortable and safe? I began my life as a male."

I have had many unique and unexpected moments in my years with CQ, but this was on a different scale altogether. The look on the team's faces, and mine, was like we were trying to work out the most complex maths equation ever created.

I think the first question was, "So the children you have, were as a father, not the mother?"'

"Yes"

It took a bit of adjustment, however our facilitator Sue Johnston just took it in her stride, while the rest of us were still trying to work this tricky equation out. From there the meeting settled and we had another productive afternoon meeting with Eva fitting in seamlessly.

The following day we had scheduled to all deliver our individual TED-style talks within the team. When it got to Eva's turn, she said that she could deliver a talk on the benefits of design thinking (that is, the procedures the designers go through), or transitioning her gender. Well, design thinking is really interesting, but it didn't have a chance against the latter subject.

The next hour was absolutely riveting, and I think I learnt more in that hour than most. Eva had realised from a very young age she was in the wrong body. At about three years of age, she told us, she'd had her first thoughts that things were not quite right.

Her partner Anne was totally accepting of the transition and supported her as she underwent the procedure. She was intensively interviewed to make sure psychologically she was up to the transition. The surgery sounded incredibly advanced and sophisticated.

I was cottoning on to the fact gender was not black or white—there are many shades and colours in between.

However, here was the most fascinating aspect for me to grasp: Society treats you with less respect as a female than as a male, especially as a professional like Eva. Many understand this already (I can be a bit naive however), but it was fascinating to hear from someone who has literally been on two sides of the gender situation.

Eva went on to become an integral part of our team, and we loved her creative genius. Being transgender was never mentioned again.

She challenged me in some unexpected way every meeting and was a force to be reckoned with. When she hosted us, we learnt how she brought huge value to her clients through design thinking. However, on her Host Day, she started complaining of a pain in her forearm. She was scheduled to get it checked out by her doctor, as it was not calming down.

That was the last meeting Eva attended. The pain she was feeling was caused by a tumour in her brain. Eva and Anne lived in Dunedin. I was in contact with Anne regularly via phone calls to see how she was tracking. When Eva was admitted to Dunedin Hospital, it took a huge load off Anne. She was physically exhausted from nursing Eva at home. I suggested I come down for a weekend and give Anne a break which she jumped at. When you have been through this before it makes it easier to step in—by this time I had already nursed three of my family with terminal cancer.

Eva was in a general ward due to overload of the hospital, but with her own room thankfully. I was to feed her, as she didn't like the hospital food. I'm terrible with food preparation.

By now the brain tumour was well advanced and while Eva looked well enough, she could only say one word: "Fuck!" It had been a word of choice before the cancer, so it wasn't a big transition. What a hilarious time we had. I'm deaf. She couldn't talk. I said if the tumour didn't kill her, my cooking would. Of course, she replied, "Fuck!"

She had a small white board she would scribble stuff on. She loved white boards. It was a Sunday afternoon, and Eva was sitting in a chair. We were running out of fucks, so she wrote, *Tell me a story.*

"What?"

Eva, shaking the white board. "Tell me a story!" she was saying.

Typical Eva, putting me on the spot. So I began a random story which I thought was quite interesting. I was about three minutes in when I heard this funny sound coming from her. She had written *BORING* on the whiteboard.

We both broke down in a fit of giggling. It was pure, childish giggling. Which is what the charge nurse walked in and witnessed. It was time for Eva to get up and get some exercise. They asked if I could help get Eva up, as they were short staffed. So I was on the left-hand side, facing backwards, lifting Eva under her arm when her blue hospital gown fell open at the back. I couldn't help myself and said, "Fuck, you've got a big arse Eva!" To which we both roared with more laughter. The poor nurse must have wondered what the hell she had walked into.

Eva's parting words were, "Fuck off." We looked at each other with teary eyes, knowing it was for the last time.

She died 10 days later.

We have a scholarship in her name—for a talented young woman, brave enough to change the world. The first recipient was Gemma Rose, whom Eva would have loved.

We have had a number of trans members. They have all been amazing people. They have all been bullied or treated poorly at some point.

I'm so pleased this year's Olympics was all about diversity. Life is so much richer, the more diverse it is!

6. Do names or labels foster a paradigm shift?

We were at an old homestead in Central Hawkes Bay called Oruawharo. A new CQ member David had just completed his timeline. The team were now interrogating his work life and how the organisation he represented was structured. It was complicated and had many layers as it was spread across the globe. It was also ancient.

"So who is the actual big boss of this huge organisation, David?" The answer was succinct and a showstopper.

"Well that would be God."

Oh yeah God. Of course.

David van Oeveren was the Archdeacon of the Oroua Parish in the Manawatū region of Aotearoa New Zealand and had taken the plunge to join one of our teams. What I absolutely love about this paradigm shift is that he could have so easily said something else. Dumbed it down. Made it less edgy.

There are people of faith the world over who do not speak of their faith in fear of being shunned. The team (many of whom were atheists) were accepting and excited to have an Archdeacon in their team. David has skills that were on show from time to time which were out-the-gate smart. He never overused them, but they were there.

David was an epic member, and I remember on his Host Day we got to interview the Bishop of Wellington. How cool is that!

He also married Kate and I and did a fair job of that!

Collective Intelligence is designed for people from any vocation.

7. What can trigger a Paradigm Shift?

Here is the shortest but one of the most apt descriptions of a paradigm change I can remember.

A founder and CEO was explaining to his team his world and how hard he worked. He was asked how many hours he worked in a typical week.

He said with pride, "On average 80 hours a week."

Across the table I saw a member, from a totally different industry, frowning.

She said, "But I thought you were good at this?".

It was the most wonderful response I can recall.

He resigned as CEO only a few months later to make way for someone more capable so he could focus on what he was best suited to. I love this stuff.

8. Authenticity and the paradigm shift

As you have already read, school was not great for me, nor me for school. Yet here I was standing in front of all the pupils, teachers and parents of Rathkeale College for prizegiving, shaking hands and giving out trophies and cups to the happy recipients. The irony!

I had been asked back to my old college to talk with the students about leadership and life. This was as part of the Sir Peter Blake Trust program, in which I had been fortunate enough to get involved. They had asked me to talk with the prefect students in Year 13. I said I would, "But only on the condition I can talk with the ratbag students as well."

They were a bit taken aback, but said, "Okay. Oh, and could you fit in the prizegiving ceremony and talk with the school as well."

So I agreed.

A few of my old school mates laughed when I told them about my invitation and one said, "Do they have any idea who they have asked?"

"Nope—no idea."

So I turned up mid-morning on a Friday and headed off to find the headmaster. Sitting outside his office was a forlorn young man with his head down. I said, "Mate, are you in the shit?"

He replied, "Yes, I am."

So I high-fived him! He looked at me like I was a loony. Fair call.

I go in and talk to the headmaster, thinking how this is a first for me: not being in trouble, but being in his office. We put a plan together, and he sends me off with a very affable teacher to talk with the Year 13 ratbags in a classroom nearby. It was classic. They are slouching away looking at me walk in with faces that say, "What does this tosser want to talk about?"

I started off saying how nice it was to be back in my old class. That they were my crowd. I talked about how school sucked and how I never really fitted in. We had a great conversation, all slouching, shooting the breeze, talking about what they wanted to do when they left school. It was grand. Halfway through, the chap that had been sitting outside the principal's office walked in. I gave him another high-five, and this time he smiled as he started to join the dots. I said I was speaking after the prize giving, and I was going to be talking to them about them, so they'd better listen up.

All too quickly the hour was up, and they shuffled out shaking my hand. Loved it.

Deep breath. Because just then came the Prefects, and top students with their blazers dripping with pins of awards and clubs to which they belonged. I needed to change gears and talk more in their language, which was totally different. School was designed for these kids, and they had made the most of this opportunity it seemed.

We were discussing what they wanted to do when they left school and all was going well, until one chap with a very shiny blazer said he wanted to get into disruptive technology. I told him that sounded cool. Then another kid jumps in and says, "Yes, and he's the Head Prefect, you know".

Speaking to the first boy, I said, "Really? You are the Head Boy?"

"Yes, I am"

I said, "Have you ever met anyone who is involved in disruptive technology?"

"No," he said. "But it sounded like I would be good at it."

"Hmmm—What have you disrupted before? "

"Um..." Nothing came to his mind.

"Well," I said, "I've just talked with the previous class and they were all about disruption." I went on to say in my time working with disruptors they were generally people who didn't follow rules, and didn't give a damn about the authorities.

He pushed back, to his credit, and we had a productive conversation with a number of the class on the subject.

Enough of the shiny jackets. It was time for lunch. Then prizegiving.

Let me be clear. Five years at secondary school, and I had never been on the stage for prize giving before. So I now shake hands with all and sundry and say, "Well done."

Then it was time for Mr Harvey (Mr Harvey!) to say a few words. The year before they had John Key, the Aotearoa New Zealand Prime Minister speak. So things were obviously going downhill at Rathkeale!

I congratulated all the boys who had received prizes, and said to all the boys who didn't, "Don't worry. No one will remember tomorrow morning." I went on and talked about how some boys are well suited to school and there was nothing wrong with that, but for many of them it didn't work so well. I said that how you do at school was not a determining factor in how you would do once you left. In fact, apart from universities, most people couldn't give a toss.

Luckily the Principal was sitting behind me so I couldn't see his face.

I said the greatest skill you could gain while at school was to learn how to get on with your mates. More importantly to learn how to get on with people that weren't your mates. That they were not going to achieve a damn thing out in the world by themselves. They would have to learn to do whatever endeavour they chose with a team of people.

That year the college was planning to build a new gymnasium and one of the Old Boys was underwriting the build. I said that 'Old Boy' was in my class, and we jostled for 22nd and 23rd place in the C stream. I said this Old Boy did not feature on any of the honour's boards at the school, but he had definitely mastered the art of working with a wide range of people.

I then finished with a shout out to the disruptors in the first group I had talked to earlier, and said I looked forward to seeing what they created in the world.

After the speech a number of parents came up and thanked me; they had boys who were not prospering at school. Another said he had two boys there, and one had got a prize and the other didn't. He thought that the message was going to help with less friction during the holiday break.

The message I got via email the next day was from a mother and Collective Intelligence member sitting in the stands. She said she and others had so enjoyed a down-to-earth speech talking about what it's really like for a big portion of boys. She also said the principal had sat there looking like he was sucking a lemon throughout my (fortunately short) speech.

It felt good to be back at Rathkeale which had sheltered me from the Crewe Murders for five years. It felt even better to be myself, knowing it wasn't going to please everyone.

It felt good to be my authentic self.

9. Helping people see themselves for what they do best

Being a Collective Intelligence member doesn't make you perfect.

A team was meeting in a provincial city location for a Host Day. They were investigating how to help their teammate with his events business. This business was doing wonderful work, but struggling with a number of issues, including that its biggest event was burning cash and had done so for quite a while. The event was a big deal on the province's calendar—a generator of national publicity, profile and revenue.

Our member would be best described as an eternal optimist and entrepreneur, but not great at detail or creating a net profit. He was also good at causing chaos—something not uncommon for entrepreneurs.

On our list to interview was the local mayor. He turned up on time and was very prim and proper in his attire and attitude. He began giving us a well-crafted speech on how wonderful this event was and how proud he was of it being hosted in their area. The team were musing and smiling to each other, and I thought that I had better cut this dialogue short, before he dug himself in further.

"Your Worship. Sorry, but we don't have much time and need to get to the crux of the matter. We know this event is burning cash, is a huge issue for the council, and our friend is a big part of the problem. We are here to help. So please, no more of the bullshit."

For a moment I thought he was going to cry. He just looked at me crestfallen, and said, "I don't know what to do."

The next 40 minutes was a frenetic question-and-answer session, with the mayor leaving feeling wrung out—but full of hope.

I don't remember a team working so hard to deliver feedback that could actually shift the dial with a complex and long-standing dilemma. But by taking a three-year view and plan, they helped the entrepreneur to see he needed to step aside from running the business and move into sales only. Sales was his thing.

Did the event turn around financially? Yes, it did. Meanwhile the mayor had a new CEO to communicate with, and it all went spiffingly. In time.

This type of paradigm shift is our bread and butter. Helping people see they are often their own worst enemy and need to step aside to allow new talent to take the helm. Personally, I have also fitted this demographic a few years back.

10. Finally, the ultimate paradigm shift—for ourselves and our planet

"Harv, I think you've been treating Collective Intelligence like a traditional farmer. What would happen if you treated CQ as a regenerative farmer would?"

This was a question (or challenge) laid down by the uber-smart Maria King, after putting Collective Intelligence through its paces being interrogated by an Impact Team for two days.

You know when someone has given you a gift of a question like that when you just can't shake it off. I couldn't shake this one off. It's been rudimentary to our new future we are imagining.

Some context: I had been a sheep and beef farmer for 30 years, and had practised the traditional methods I had learnt at Lincoln University all those years ago. It's about control—creating predictable and measurable outcomes that bank managers really like. It's also a very Western view of the world—one in which we humans determine what's best for us and the earth.

However, I have totally flipped my view of my old farming practices and set about unlearning how to control the soil and farm. Instead, on our wee block Kate and I call Raumai Iti, we have transitioned to using regenerative agricultural methods—methods in which Māori are well versed.

So with this reverberating in my ears and heart, I have been inspired by this challenge.

Here's a definition of regenerative agriculture from the sage Jules Matthews (commonly thought of as one of the leading lights in the development of regenerative farming in Aotearoa New Zealand):

To start, let's define regenerative ag in the simplest terms. It is about improving the whole system function. This includes our natural

161

ecosystem, financial integrity as well as the social and personal aspects of a farming enterprise. Ideally, we will allow guiding principles to be applied in local contexts encouraging ingenuity, adaptability and the full capacity of human creativity. Regenerative ag is not an end goal but a journey of syntropic improvement as we look to restore the balance and function of the world that supports our existence. It is a principle-based approach to farming rather than a rule-based system such as organics. It is measured by outcomes including and not limited to water cycle function, nutrient cycling, biodiversity, animal wellbeing, food quality, economic integrity and social health. It involves a shift from viewing land as a commodity belonging to us to seeing it as a community which we belong to. Our job is to grow our understanding and connectivity both with the environment and within ourselves.

Fuck, that's a mouth full.

What Matthews has left out is the role of diversity in creating a regenerative ecosystem.

So many Western models of commerce, governance, education and caring for our planet are just not working. We talk of sustainability when we are not in a sustainable world.

To have a world where humanity and other current life forms can exist on this planet means we are going to have to learn to be regenerative in all aspects of our life.

This is what we are imagining as we go forward with Collective Intelligence: To create regenerative ecosystem for people who care enough to help each other to do great work.

I believe that trust is the life blood of this ecosystem we want to create, flowing through our veins. More of this in the next book.

Reflections:

- This chapter sums up much of the learnings from my life and experiences with Collective Intelligence. Rather than pose a reflective question or two, could I ask you to skim back through the ten paradigm shift stories which could relate to your own and what you may have learnt from them?

- Thank you for reading this far. The following and final chapter talks about the future of Collective Intelligence and our new, exciting initiatives of which I'd invite you to participate.

Chapter 18

Collective Intelligence: The Futures—
Bringing potential into the world

"How can Collective Intelligence honour Te Tiriti o Waitangi as a private company, Harv?"

And the afternoon had been going so well.

"I have no idea, Riana. How?"

"Well, no one seems to know at the moment—but if anyone can work it out, you lot can."

This was the challenge put down by Riana Manuel. We were at an Auckland meeting, organised to informally catch up with CQ alumni and members.

As it happened, I was travelling to Hamilton the next morning and got in contact with Che Wilson to join me for breakfast and relayed the challenge Riana had set down.

"How can Collective Intelligence honour Te Tiriti o Waitangi as a private company, Che?"

In typical Che fashion, he says, "Hmmm. I will need to channel into the ancestors".

So here I am, in a café on a Friday morning while Che is sitting there, his arms spread wide, eyes closed and he's chanting in a low voice while channelling his ancestors. White boy Harv over the other side of the table was feeling a bit uncomfortable, and then relieved when he stopped.

"Nothing there", he proclaimed, and then says we need a hui.

So a hui (meeting) was organised with some of our sage Māori members of the Collective Intelligence ecosystem in Wellington. When I look back at the depth of wisdom assembled that day, it makes me shudder with pride and just how privileged I am.

Che was presenting at Parliament that day and turned up in traditional Māori piupiu (skirt). Anake Goodal had flown in from Christchurch, Bettina Anderson and Peter Butler had travelled with me from Palmerston North, Riana from Coromandel, Erin Wansbrough from Hamilton, and Amy McClean patched in via zoom. We started with the traditional pepeha (a way of acknowledging and honouring your connection to the land and their ancestors) then framing up of why we were there.

The kōrero (conversation) quickly turned to the fact that the Treaty of Waitangi/Te Tiriti o Waitangi had not been honoured by the Crown, and the energy in the room ramped up big time. Lots of emotion, anger, frustration and feelings of betrayal were all put out on the table. Being Pākehā in the presence of this energy, I personally felt overwhelmed by the outpouring of grief from the Māori in the room.

Then out of nowhere came a comment about developing cultural intelligence and working effectively across culturally diverse situations, since, to those present, the Treaty is about inclusivity. A light bulb went off in my mind.

"To develop cultural intelligence you would first need to be conscious that there are in fact other cultures," I started. "Then you would need to become curious about those other cultures. Being curious is great—however, you then need to become courageous to do something about the curiosity. Then you may become competent in the culture."

Everyone stopped and looked at me, and Anake said, "That's how you honour Te Tiriti O Waitangi!"

The tension in the room melted before me.

It was a very odd feeling and one on which I still can't put my finger. But it was out in the open.

Being *conscious*—getting *curious*—then a little *courageous*—and becoming *competent*. What I absolutely love about this framework is that it's a beginner's mindset and ends up being an infinity loop. You can progress to 'competent', fall off, and then start again. I have seen this happen numerous times as we explore new cultures as a company, or facilitator, or as an individual.

At no stage do you become an expert or say, "I know the way!"

Cultural intelligence, I believe, is just too complex and subtle for the expert mindset.

We finished the hui early, as it was clear we had identified how to honour the Treaty. I said to Che, "That was intense, bro".

He smiled and said, "We knew if you came under enough pressure it would surface".

What has transpired is that this now forms the basis of our methodology for all our work: the beginners or learners mindset. This cultural intelligence framework is the core of all models we are developing for individuals or organisations.

Individual Development Methodology

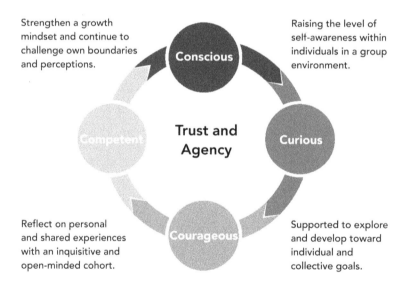

Strengthen a growth mindset and continue to challenge own boundaries and perceptions.

Raising the level of self-awareness within individuals in a group environment.

Conscious

Competent

Trust and Agency

Curious

Courageous

Reflect on personal and shared experiences with an inquisitive and open-minded cohort.

Supported to explore and develop toward individual and collective goals.

© 2024 Collective Intelligence—Developed by Kim Aitken & Dr. Amanda Evans

It makes me wonder what Aotearoa New Zealand would be like today if the Crown had honoured the Treaty in the first place. We have a chance to make up for lost time, and I know Māori are moving at pace to make the most of the Treaty settlements. I just hope Pākehā can keep up.

I hear the fear some Pākehā have of the rise of Māoridom. My view is they are worried because they are looking through the lens of a Western framework, colonisation and dominance—one that views cultures as competing rather than working together. I encourage Pākehā to learn Te ao Māori which emphasises the importance of relationships between nature and people. It is a holistic worldview that focuses on interconnections and is grounded in tikanga customary values and lore and mātauranga (knowledge and wisdom).

There is nothing to fear. There is so much to learn. When we do, our nation will have a flourishing cultural intelligence the rest of the world will envy!

We have more in common with the 'other' than not. This poem from one of our Collective Intelligence alumni Alina Siegried expresses my view better than I ever could.

A Cure for Them
By Alina Siegfried

If we are to believe the stories that dominate our social media feed,
there are an evil group of people out there
who are out to destroy our lives.

They do not share our values,
they have no common sense,
they will take away your freedom, bombard you with fake news.
Brainwashing your children with their propaganda,
they will do everything in their power
to take away all that you hold sacred.

Beware, they are out there,
the people we call
"Them"

Them, the enemy,
them, those other ones,

them, the ones we must overcome,
the target of every comment section,
everywhere

So confident are we
that we are the ones who are right,
we have turned respectful public debate
into millions of miniature, individual dictatorships of the mind.
The teeth of our savage sound bites grow ever sharper by the day
while indignant ears remain deaf to anything
that does not reinforce our worldview.

There is no room for reason in a lynch mob,
no longer a gift in give and take.
No space for context and complexity in a 280-character tweet.
The air is growing thin in this here echo chamber,
it's getting harder and harder to breathe.

We need not even look too far before we can identify a "them."
Even amongst brothers and sisters in arms,
sibling rivalry cuts deep.

The climate activist questions the urgency of queer rights if we have
no habitable planet to call our home.
The unionist challenges foreign aid when a working wage can't even
feed our own people.
We hear, it's the immigrants who are the problem,
or those people in SUVs.
It's the dairy farmers, the greenies, the feminists, the TERFs,
the bankers, the church, the NRA.
It's corporate welfare, guerrilla warfare,
it's the liberal media, the gay agenda,
it's them,
it's they,
it's those people,
if only they would . . . Stop!

Listen.
Can you hear that?

That is the sound of singular stories.
It's the sound of petty distractions.
It's the sound of red herrings gasping for breath
as the future slips away.

Oblivious to our own hypocrisy and wasting our precious energy,
we are setting ourselves on fire in the hopes that
they will die of smoke inhalation.

It need not be this way.
We can be better than this.
We have the cure for "them,"
it's simple.
It is us.

What if we took our pointing fingers, and we turned them upside
down
to extend the gentle hand of compromise?
Offered up our gifts and contributions with open hearts,
embracing grace and humility?

That's not to say that we should deny the role of privilege,
ignore the wounds from the past,
or cease to pursue our passion for change.
After all, even the Buddha taught non-violence, not pacifism.
But let us dismantle systems of oppression
without creating carbon copies addressed to "them."

Step away from the militancy you have held so close,
as a lover.
Soften your heart and walk a mile in shoes that do not fit,
shoes that cause you discomfort,

blisters edging their way in
beneath the soles of the feet you have so firmly planted
in the arguments you have convinced yourself are solid.
This place is familiar, it is comfortable.
But we desperately need to stand upon
common ground.

For it is there that we can pinpoint the underlying causes
behind our addiction to outrage.
Feelings of grief, of losing that which we hold dear.
Feelings of fear, of those who we do not understand.
Feelings of pain, of leaning into the despair of not knowing
how the hell we are going to
get ourselves out of this mess.

Respect the collective wisdom that comes from listening
to many voices that are different from your own.
Find your passion,
and then you do you, and do it well,
while simultaneously seeking to understand
why it is that they care so much about something else.

According to particle physics,
we exchange 98 percent of the atoms in our bodies
with the world around us every year.

So I am you,
and you are me.
And they are us.
And we are them.

We are them.
We are them.
To somebody, somewhere,
you are them.

Building a new future starts now

There's a quote from Buckminster Fuller that I love, because that exemplifies some of the work we have undertaken recently: "You never change things by fighting the existing reality. To change something, build a new model that makes the existing model obsolete."

About three years ago, I was approached by a chap to help him with a big idea he had. Could we help him? I liked the idea and could see the potential. I said, "Let's give it a go," and curated a diverse team of people who were drawn to the idea. We worked with him for about seven months, meeting once a week online to help keep him on track and develop the concept, and it didn't work out. Gutted.

However, like all failures, that is where the learning comes from. And we learnt a lot! As it turns out that was just as well, as we were soon to trial the model again.

Only a month later I was introduced by Sarah Tocker to Dr Amanda Evans, a smart and passionate paediatric palliative care specialist, who also had a big idea. Once again, I was intrigued and wanted to help. Each year, 280 families have terminally sick children, and Amanda was frustrated with the care they got in Aotearoa New Zealand.

When I was sure Amanda was up for it, I curated a new team, and away we went helping Amanda to bring her idea to life. Same routine, meeting regularly online, and then in person. This time it worked, and today a new prototype is up and running. The Government has a chance now to take notice and implement this nationally to create a gold standard for paediatric palliative care. If they don't, then it's on them!

We then undertook another project and wrapped around Kim Aitken, who has developed a new method of building homes that are warmer, cooler, put together faster, meet most passive standards, and are cost effective. It's called Truss House, and it's a game changer.

The diverse CQ team we curated once again challenged and supported her, also having a ball and helping bring this tangible creation to fruition.

There is one instance that stands out in this particular process with

Kim, that is significant. I got a call one December morning from a distressed Kim saying that the intellectual property was about to be exposed, as a deal they had been working on had evaporated at the last minute. In three working days, the latest iteration of the new plans would not be protected anymore.

I asked, "What do you need?"

She said, "I need to be able to register this plan for a building project by Wednesday next week".

"Leave it with me."

So I rang a long standing CQ member Mark Hamilton of Alexander Construction in Hawkes Bay and told him the dilemma. He asked some questions, and said it was possible in a pinch. Long story short, two strangers had it nailed down by Tuesday. At the time, there was nothing in it for Mark, other than helping out another CQ member he didn't know. Kim later said to me that "it's like I have bunch of capable strangers who I can trust implicitly."

What if we develop an ecosystem built on trust?

The world moves at the speed of trust. Trust is based on the actions of people. Brené Brown has the best framework I have seen on what it takes to build trust. She calls it BRAVING, which stand for:

- Boundaries
- Reliability
- Accountability
- Vault
- Integrity
- Non Judgement
- Generosity

Mark Hamilton and Kim Aitken exuded all of these elements during their time working together. It's something we are consciously building on today as we move forward with Collective Intelligence, too. The CQ Incubator process established a partnership model that demonstrates how values-driven businesses can align to create meaningful impact.

As I write, there are the first tranche of Truss Houses being built. Some by Alexander Construction. I love shit like this emerging!

We have called this initiative 'Incubator Teams', and it is showing huge promise to make the changes about which Buckminster Fuller was quoted earlier.

The two diagrams below taken from Matthew Syed's 2019 book *Rebel Ideas* show exactly what we try to achieve. Wrapping a diverse team around ambitious and intelligent people like Amanda and Kim.

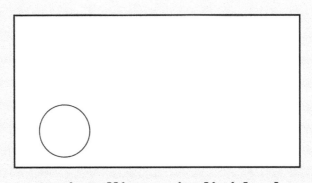

An intelligent individual

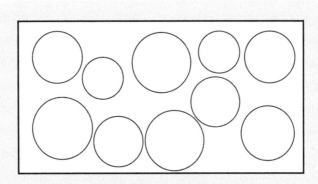

An intelligent team
(A team of rebels)

Incubator Teams

Old systems are getting in the way of progress, and this is how we want to help out—by creating new paradigms. This is our jam! Fuck the systems that aren't serving us, and instead build something generative.

Getting teams to hum!

What is not easily understood, and hard to express, is how to get the diverse teams humming. I've given this a lot of thought over the years.

A diverse team is like a band. These bands are into riffing, which is where they are interacting with each other, innovating based on an existing tune or progression. It's a term also used in comedy, where a performer might improvise around a subject or theme. Whether in comedy or music, the idea is to create a fresh, collaborative and spontaneous performance.

Nick Granville is a friend and professional guitarist, and he explained to me that there is always a leader when riffing, but the audience can't always tell who that leader is. He went on to say that the key to riffing is observing and listening intently to what the other band members are doing, and not dominating. Every musician has a place, and you're listening to create. One of my all-time favourite pieces of musical riffing is from 'Little Red Roster—Wowling Wolf London Sessions' with Eric Clapton. Steve Winwood, Bill Wyman and Charlie Watt. Enjoy!

Something that is so easily overlooked in a team is the need to create space for the quiet people. You have to work hard and observe when they want to speak, and then be patient. Reflective thinkers, and introverts *must* have a say. In *Better*, Christina Wedgwood cites Adam Grant's description of the 'babble effect', where often the noisy people are listened to more, as people assume they know what they are talking about. They don't.

I have been a babbler. I am growing out of it. I prefer to listen to others more than talking. When I am asked to give a speech, I will engage the audience as quickly as possible and construct a conversation, rather than just giving a speech. It's better for everyone. A couple of years ago, I gave a presentation to a group about the importance of the B Corp movement. I was to speak before dinner, which I did, engaging the crowd in dialogue. As it turned out they asked me to continue talking after dinner as well, for a total of just over two hours. It was a blast, and they said it was the best speech they had been given in the 12 years the organisation had been meeting. Why? Because they talked more than me.

At Collective Intelligence, everyone is expected to talk in their team, to contribute, to listen, to be okay with riffing.

I bring this up now because Lara Blackmore, whom I have the pleasure to work alongside, has said recently we need to teach people how to build their own diverse teams. She's right. We are currently working on how to deliver that to a wide range of organisations. Lara is also excellent at riffing, and bonus points she is also a synthesiser, or alchemist if you prefer. Most of our methodology has been glued together by Lara. It was instigated by Chris Gallavin (a very smart dude), but it needed Lara to bring it into the light of day.

Following is some of her work, which is genius in that it uses so few words. I start reading at the top and slowly work my way to the bottom, and I am filled with hope and possibility of what collectivism can achieve. I love the diagram on the following page and will be eternally grateful to Lara for putting it all together.

At Collective Intelligence

We believe there's a better way

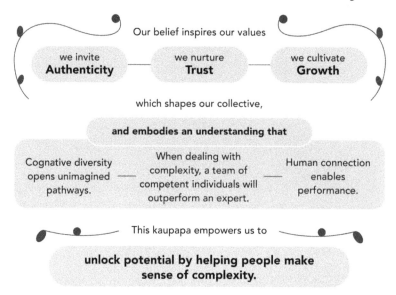

Our belief inspires our values

we invite
Authenticity

we nurture
Trust

we cultivate
Growth

which shapes our collective,

and embodies an understanding that

Cognative diversity opens unimagined pathways.

When dealing with complexity, a team of competent individuals will outperform an expert.

Human connection enables performance.

This kaupapa empowers us to

unlock potential by helping people make sense of complexity.

On reading the draft of this final chapter, Lara commented:

> I've been with Collective Intelligence for a year, as a member, an employee and now as CE. I came in during Harv's sabbatical, when the business was in the hands of some trusted friends. What I have been involved in, alongside Harv since he returned, has been a process of healing and elevation of our awareness of what Collective Intelligence is, how it interacts in the world and its potential to create impact. Much like the journey of our members, we have come through the discomfort of the darkness, the space where growth happens, and into the light. We believe there's a better way and it is our purpose to unlock potential by helping people make sense of complexity. It's enduring and it's what the world needs right now. And I love the potential we are bringing into the world.

Lara mentions my sabbatical in her comments. Well, last year I suffered burnout—one that had its roots in 2019 with five surgeries, then dealing with the fallout from Covid. This is the abbreviated version, obviously. So the team gave me time off work, and I went off to do some manual work and get some sunlight on my face.

I spent the first two weeks of my break catching up at home and pruning people's trees around the North Island. It was a tonic to be outside and doing the kind of physical work I love. One spring morning on Waiheke Island, I got to chatting with Manda Jane Johnson over breakfast; I had been pruning her fruit trees for a couple of days. I stated that I have noticed people don't often truly see trees until they are a problem. I went on to muse that I love looking at trees and seeing how they are, wondering if they need attention or companion plants around them, and so on. Manda said, "Well, Harv, you are a bit like that with people too."

It's amazing what comes out of her mouth at times.

Over this sabbatical, I had the chance to work on two of our CQ members' businesses. One was a vineyard in Hawkes Bay, driving a wee blue tractor; the other was pruning trees on a farm in Whitemans Valley, Wellington. It was so good to move the old body again.

The biggest benefit, though, was to work in a team again, on the bottom rung of the ladder. It was fascinating with all the experience of my past years' knowledge, yet being out of the management loop. What I saw was illuminating and has sparked another new initiative. There's nothing like getting up close and personal for me to learn and relearn new things.

What stood out to me was the guys on the ground were not being listened to by those higher up the hierarchy, and it was causing frustration and lethargy. Working inside both businesses, I noticed a disconnect between people within the team. Sometimes that was because of distance, time constraints, different paradigms. The modern business world is rapidly changing, in tandem with cultural changes and the uprooting of a traditional, patriarchal system (remember the GWM). This means leadership techniques have to adapt, away from the traditional methods of patriarchal hierarchy, which are often described as being elitist, secretive and bureaucratic.

So, after a number of conversations with one of the owners, I was considering if we might be able to take our core business of curating diverse teams to make sense of complexity inside a business, and work with the whole workforce.

I started talking with facilitators about it, and Penny Cooper introduced me to the work Sidney Yoshida had done in 1989. Yoshida found that, even though 100 percent of front-line problems were known to the front-line employees, only 74 percent were known to team leaders, nine percent to middle management, and just four percent to top management!

He coined the term the 'Iceberg of Ignorance'. Now, I'm not sure if these numbers are still true today, but I would say the ratios would not have altered significantly and are still relevant.

This is what I was seeing while being on the ground floor. So then I had to ask the question of how to melt the iceberg. Apparently, the answer is humility.

There's a magic that happens when a bunch of strangers on our CQ teams get together and start sharing intimately. The question was this: Could we replicate this in an organisation where everyone works together and knows each other?

I needed a brave business leader to let us trial the concept. It took only a few months before the opportunity arose with Jamie Storey, CEO of warehousing business Chemcare based in South Auckland, and a CQ member for about 10 years now. He was sharing his frustrations with me. He didn't know what was going through the minds of the team on the ground floor—a team made up of 50 or so people from at least a dozen nationalities. Jamie wanted to create a flat, non-hierarchical structure, but was flummoxed on how to achieve this.

I prodded more and kept listening. I needed to be sure before I blundered in with my idea, and didn't want to kill the moment. I talked about my experience the year before, and then my solution of creating CQ Teams within a business. Jamie just sat there pondering (he's good at that) and showed no emotion or response. Then he started asking questions. Lots of questions.

Today, we are underway with a three-year program, and the big question has been answered. We have been able to create *enough* of the magic that is created in our CQ Teams. Already I can see the iceberg melting in front of us. After three years, Chemcare will be a vastly different company to work within. Thank you, Jamie, for giving it a go.

Lara has been adamant that there is an opportunity for us to help organisations after they have been through a restructure, lift teams' trust levels, build confidence in themselves, and help them gain clarity of what the future looks like. I think she is right. As I write this, we now have two more companies about to get started. This makes my heart sing.

As a nation, we seem to care more about and understand more about developing sports teams than we do about caring for teams at work. This needs to be reversed. I have said this often in recent months as I have been studying this iceberg. Too many of our organisation and corporate frameworks in particular have been copied from army principles. No more. We need organisations to be designed to maximise Collective Intelligence.

Impact Teams

Some years back, one of our members, who had been a senior partner in one of the Big Four consulting companies, sat down with me to discuss transferring our methodology into the consulting space. It wasn't a foreign concept to me; I had been thinking along the same lines for a while. What was a surprise was being endorsed by someone from inside that world.

We found a company willing to trial the idea. We curated a suitable Impact Team from inside the CQ membership and set up a process to put this company under extensive scrutiny for a few days. The team members had never worked together before, but you would have never guessed it. They were riffing like Clapton and Howlin' Wolf!

The chap from the Big Four was in the team and it was great to get his perspective and compare the results to what he and his consultancy were used to. The team smashed it! They gave great value and had a ball. I'm not going into detail here as it breaches confidentiality and some of our IP. However, we went on and ran number of more trials, all working well.

Right now we are hoping to kick off a major project with an organisation that wants to push the envelope. They are wrapping up some old ways of operating, and don't have a clear view of what needs to be created for the future. They have come to Collective Intelligence as they have heard of our work and believe we can help them. We can.

Impact Teams has been a slow burn and is now ready to roll. The world needs new ways of operating, and while we are not consultants, we are ready to move into this space with confidence. We have literally hundreds of trained alumni waiting to be activated. This would be a dream come true for me.

However, at the heart of our work are the CQ teams where we continue to support individuals on their unique journeys. This will always be at the heart of what we do.

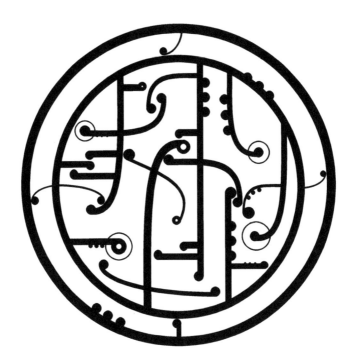

"Te mauri kei roto"

Here, "mauri" refers to a life force, essence, or energy, which aligns with the meaning of "magic" within a deeper, spiritual context.

Here's a Māori interpretation from artist, Peter Butler:

> The concept/theme of the design that came to mind when designing this was 'the magic within'—the magic/mauri that happens when CQ teams operate and function well, as well as exploring that which is within us all, once we focus and channel our inner mauri!

This speaks to my heart!

Final reflections

We push forward. But how do we reimagine a future that is not just sustainable, but actually generative, or better still regenerative? What models can we observe and learn from that will build a future where my moko (grandchildren) and their moko can live in a place in harmony with the world around them?

Nature is the answer. Observing how plants, insects and indigenous animals interact with each other to create a future. If I had any advice to young professionals starting out today, is to go study the ngahere (Aotearoa New Zealand's native forests) where trees, mosses, fungi, birds, insects and shrubs are all interconnected and rely on each other to thrive. They share resources in times of scarcity. And that's what we need to do as a society.

I have written this book for young people starting out in their careers, thinking of myself when I was starting out, and what I would tell myself. This was a young man that would never believe he would one day be able to write a book worth reading.

The message is this: Please do not look at the shiny leader, or person with a big stack of possessions, and wish, *that's what I want.* Please do not compare yourself with others. (It's hard not to.) Remember, after working with over a thousand so-called successful people from across many industries, as it turns out they do not have their shit together either.

There's a better way. Be yourself. It's more than enough. You are more than enough.

Thank You All . . .

There have been several people over the years who have left an indelible stamp on the way we have tried to mould Collective Intelligence. It's appropriate at this point in the book, to reflect on some that have stood out, and tell a little of their stories.

I had the pleasure to work with and be mentored by Keith Mason, AKA The Purple Guy, who mentors people to improve their emotional communication, and empower and transform their personal and business/team relationships. It was a big stretch for me at the time, but I learnt a huge amount from him. He would talk about what he loved most about Collective Intelligence: that we did not try and pretend we had the answers. We encouraged our members to think for themselves and encouraged a wide range of views, rather than mould anyone into this—the way it should be done.

In our early years, we had a member who owned a construction company in Christchurch. He was adamant that he never wanted to find that some bank, consulting firm, or accountancy was behind the scenes, financing and manipulating how CQ operated. He was rather staunch on this view. It resonated with me, and while it would have been welcome to have that financial support at times, it has meant we have been able to sense and respond to our members as we thought best. It's given us freedom to create, and we have made the most of that freedom

Mary Beth Robles came out of the blue. A New Yorker, Mary Beth had come from a corporate background, working for Colgate in many countries before taking the CEO position of Colgate New Zealand. She came on board as our own CEO for a couple of years and was a gift to be able to work alongside so much experience and wisdom. Mary Beth taught me many things. The one that stands out the most was the advice on my succession plan, when she said, "Do not look to one person as your succession plan. Rather, look for a number of people as a combination". That's sage advice, and we are looking right now how that might be formulated.

Maryanne Bevin believed in the future of Collective Intelligence before anyone else, maybe even me. She pushed and pushed us to lift our game, asked for more, for better, and we responded. Thank you.

During the course of helping write a speech, Michael Philpott un-covered my personal 'Why'. I thought I had it, but I was wrong. Michael is a professional speech writer, amongst other things, and shared his 'Why'. By doing that, he unlocked my mind. During the aftermath of the Crewe Murders, my extended family were not able to rest nor properly mourn this terrible loss. We didn't have the facts. What Michael allowed me to see clearly is that Collective Intelligence brings me joy when our members receive unbiased, clear information via their Collective Intelligence team.

Today, I can proudly say that my 'Why' is for members to gain unbi-ased information so they can take action with the wisdom of their Col-lective Intelligence Team. Now I understand it, I relish witnessing when I see this in action. I wished my family had more support when they needed it most, but I can't change that now. But I can support others.

The work I do with Collective Intelligence helps heal the wounds from my childhood and is the reason why I continue when everything gets me down. But it also needs to be remembered that this is my per-sonal 'Why' and needs to be kept in proportion with the greater mission of helping members on their own journey—whether that is spurring them on or helping them to change course. The hardest part is often just making things actually happen at all. We love it all!

Ross Herbert, whom I mentioned in Chapter 3, has had a huge im-pact on me. He's inspired me to take on new skills as I get older, to keep developing and creating more neural pathways. I started sculpting in my 30s and have continued to this day. I didn't start playing golf until I was 53 years of age, and in my 66th year I'm trying to get my handi-cap down to single figures for the first time. This has all stemmed from Ross's influence, I can now see. Maybe Collective Intelligence would not have been born without his influence.

Finally, Bob Selden has been my editor, and rock throughout the journey of writing this book, coaching me about storytelling, and most of all keeping me enthusiastic about the project. I had a wobble in the middle, and felt like no one would ever read this shit. His reply was bril-liant: "Yes, we all get to this space when writing a book, and I give you two days to shake it off and get going again". So I did.

I have also been amazed by what I had forgotten along the way, and what I have made sense of by putting things down on paper. Writing about Dominion Breweries—their buying our family business the Tui Brewery, the subsequent damage they created to the natural environment including cutting the oaks, and disregard to the whakapapa in the name of mass producing beer—was a slow creep. On reflection, the culmination felt like we had been invaded, or maybe a form of colonisation. This is a new reflection for me. It has made me wonder if that is why I have such a strong connection and empathy with Māori.

This journey has been windy, fun and fraught at times, with many challenges.

Without great governance Collective Intelligence would not exist today. Special thanks to our Board Chairs over the years:

John Barber
Stephen McPhail
Bobbie O'Fee
Matthew Doyle
Margaret Kouvelis
Wendy Alexander

You all know how much you have contributed on the journey keeping Collective Intelligence on track. It's not always easy dealing with a Founder who gets distracted easily. But you did it anyway.

To the very small group of personal friends who have supported me behind the scenes for years, hearing my joy and angst, and treating them all the same. You know who you are—I say thank you.

My Collective Intelligence team along the way, seeing me struggle and struggle with the lack of many things. Answering my question 'Should I give up'? With a consistent—No! Helping me to keep my eyes up and seeing the potential on the horizon. You lot know exactly what it's taken;

Terry, Pauline, Matt, Alex, Rod, Jamie, Alana, Sasha, Maria, Andy, Kim, Iain, and Kylie—thanks Team!

To the team of facilitators who have brought so much knowledge and experience into the world of Collective Intelligence and moulded how our CQ teams work.

Pamela Meekings-Stewart
Sue Johnston
Manda Johnson
Pete Swinburn
Meg Rose
Sarah Tocker
Kathy Tracey
Lisa Markwick
Dallis Parker
John Lasenby
Adam Cooper

What a talented, amazing list of Facilitators. I'm so humbled you all chose to work with me.

To Chris Gallavin and Lara Blackmore for turning up at exactly the right time so I could stay on sabbatical.

To my kids, Gabby, Guy and Daniel for accepting the transition your old man went through in reimaging his future. For just being in the world as your own people, becoming awesome parents and adults. I feel a huge sense of pride watching you grow up.

To my wife Kate. I doubt this is what you signed up for, however, whenever I needed your support, there it was. Collective Intelligence would not exist today without you. My most poignant memory was sitting on the side of the bed at 4.30am in the morning, with a tough day ahead. I let out a sigh. Your response was classic, "Get up. Get dressed. Go do your work".

I promise to get my shit together soon.

References

Foreword

Clarkson's Farm —a British television documentary series about Jeremy Clarkson and his farm in the Cotswolds https://www.imdb.com/title/tt10541088/

Introduction

The Chatham House Rule —used to encourage inclusive and open dialogue in meetings. https://www.chathamhouse.org/about-us/chatham-house-rule

Chapter 1

Report of the Royal Commission to Inquire into the Circumstances of the Convictions of Arthur Allan Thomas for the Murders of David Harvey Crewe and Jeanette Lenore Crewe 1980.

Chapter 8

Rosenberg, Marshall B. Nonviolent Communication: A Language of Compassion. ebrandedbooks.com. US 2003.

Chapter 11

Collins, J.C. Good to Great: Why Some Companies Make the Leap... and Others Don't. Random House Business, 2001.

Chapter 13

Brown, B. Dare to Lead: Brave Work. Tough Conversations. Whole Hearts. Random House Business, 2018.

Chapter 14

Hannant, A. Why social enterprise is a good idea, and how we can get more of it. TED Talk https://www.youtube.com/watch?v=Kx9tizvS8NY

Guenther, A. How crowdfunding is going to change the world: TED Talk https://www.youtube.com/watch?v=F1_viddQGSQ

B Corp Movement. Make Business a Force For Good. https://www.bcorporation.net/en-us/

Chapter 15

Consedine, R & J. Healing Our History: the challenge of the Treaty of Waitangi. Penguin, 2012.

Chapter 16

Dylan, B. The Times They are a Changin. https://www.youtube.com/watch?v=TlPV4wtZ6HE

Kelly, B. Deputy Chief Executive Officer/Chief Information Officer. Tertiary Education Commission 2014-19.

Chapter 17

Syed, M. Rebel Ideas: The Power of Diverse Thinking. John Murray Publishers, 2019.

Collective Intelligence is a diverse,
one-of-a-kind human ecosystem that takes inspiration
from Mother Nature to grow more grounded people,
more emotionally intelligent leaders and more
future-focused and resourceful communities.

For more information go to:

www.collectiveintelligence.co.nz

And to contact us:

community@collectiveintelligence.co.nz

Testimonials

'I meet a lot of people lost in their leadership roles, I recognise myself in them until Collective Intelligence took me in.'
Brian Hendersen, Banker

'Harv approaches life with a raw honesty, insatiable curiosity and funnybone humour that gently unfurls truth amidst pretension. He's like whiskey and honey: raw, earthy authenticity that strips out bullshit, followed by a balm of humour and wisdom. A joy to know!'
Rosalie Nelson, CEO Edmund Hillary Fellowship

'Harv is a clear shooter—looking for that new way to connect people rather than using the old 'Number 8 wire' approach. In particular, Harv's ability to build relationships where people can unbundle complexity which helps create a non-threatening place from which to grow—our 'Aotearoa Hou'—our place to bind together.

In my experience as a past CQ team member, I've seen Harv navigate topics and issues that what too many people might see as threatening or they'd rather sweep under the carpet. His gift is so simple—a sense of collectivism moving away from what some would describe as "selfish bastards" always looking for me, myself, I, to what can be achieved by working together where all can reap opportunity and/or benefit.

Harv has an ability to apologise when he stuffs up, which shows one of his true characteristics—humility through empathy. This builds stronger relationships and people describe him as a "good bugger with a modern edge".

In Harv's embracement of Māori culture, I can see him telling the dominant groups—in the case of Aotearoa, Pakeha, that it's OK to take a collective approach and not to be scared of change—not to see it as a threat, but to embrace an 'Aotearoa Hou' together while continuing to move forward.'
Che Wilson, Poukura (director) of Naia Limited

'In a complex time where information is confused with connection, CQ is the grounding force of honesty and aroha that reminds me I'm not alone in my fight to build a better world.'

Alana Alan—Business and Advertising Director

'CQ for me represents all the best things about being a human. In a world where we are increasingly disconnected and fed information that reinforces our existing views, CQ provides a level of connection, challenge, safety and care that nurtures curiosity and hope.'

Sasha Lockley, Co-Founder of Money Sweet Spot

'My time in Collective Intelligence reminded me of a fundamental truth that many of us have forgotten... that true intelligence comes in many forms—head, heart, body and spirit.

And while we sometimes navigate the lessons of life in the most messy, ineloquent and ungraceful of ways, it's been a true gift to have a team of like-hearted people who will hold your hand as you walk through the fire while never hesitating to call you out the moment they sense that you're kidding yourself.'

Alina Siegfried—Author, Storyteller, Narrative Specialist

'A unique combination of intense curiosity and broad life experience, married with brutal honesty and an appetite to rethink the way we engage with the world around us, makes Harv the most constructive disrupter that I've had the privilege of meeting.'

Dr Rich Laing

About the Author

Harv is the product of family and societal norms not quite coming together as they should. As a result he seldom aspired to go with the staus quo. In fact he often went out of his way to challenge the systems he thought were not serving society. It would be fare to say he has annoyed more people than he can remember. His Father Bill would say he was a cross-grained bastard at times.

Today Harv lives on a 8 ha wee farm of sand country west of Bulls, with his wife Kate, three horses, three cats.

After 6 years of regenerative farming practices he is learning that he knows so little about the soil. He's also a fungi junky.